Multicultural Books
to Make and Share
Easy-to-Make • Authentic • Cross-Curricular

Susan Kapuscinski Gaylord

D1377487

S C H O L A S T I C
PROFESSIONAL BOOKS

New York • Toronto • London • Sydney • Auckland

Copyright © 1994 by Susan Kapuscinski Gaylord
Cover and interior design by Vincent Ceci
Interior illustration by Susan Kapuscinski Gaylord
Cover illustrations by Mario Angeloni, Alexis Wile, Kara Hutchinson, David Clay, Hillary Foster, Kenny Allison

0-590-49821
Printed in U.S.A.
12 11 10 9 8 7 6 5 4 3 2 1

for my parents
with love and gratitude

Alfred John Kapuscinski
and
Helen Jean Donahue Kapuscinski
(in memoria)

Credits:

Photographs of student work by James Higgins

Name Scroll, page 23:
Alexander Vallejo, Heather Dwan, Abbey Coviello

Zulu Beadwork, page 29:
Megan Burritt, Mario Angeloni, Lauren Hersey, Kristin Mahoney

Wish Scroll, page 35:
Lindsay Jones, John Giglio

Adinkra Cloth, page 39:
Kathryn Wecal, Steven Longworth, Kate Dore

Winter Count, page 49:
Kara Hutchinson

Time Line Accordion, page 53:
Ryan Shephard, Ashley Hotz

Comic Book, page 59:
Daniel Juralewicz, Elizabeth Vetne, Katie Vespa

Curandero Book, page 63:
Alexis Wile, Caitlin Cooper, Noel Roycroft

Palm Leaf Sequence Book, page 75:
Jonathan Powers, Stephanie Camerlengo, Tracy Twombly, Douglas Standley

Math Slat Book, page 79:
Kenny Allison, Brian Carey, Kellie Hunter

Seasons Accordion Book, page 83:
Gary Twombly, Danielle Arciero

Book of Haiku, page 91:
Rachel Wintner, Jessie Bryan, Alaina Markos

Runes, page 105:
Jared Gordon, Ryan Erhardt, Stacey Allaire

Pugillares, page 109:
Jordan Ignacio, Jennifer Wilmot, Molly Edson

Newsbook, page 113:
Alexander Thompson, David Clay, Hillary Foster

Medieval Book, page 119:

Steven Alicea, Shauna Bedrosian, Lisa McGregor

Poetry by Paul Marion
"Haiku for Hurricane Coup," p. 93,
© 1992 by Paul Marion, used with permission of the author

"Rain Sings," p. 94,
© 1976 by Paul Marion, used with permission of the author

Table of Contents

Acknowledgements

This book is, in many ways, a summary of my work with teachers and students for the past five years. It has developed in several phases: researching different book forms from around the world, adapting them to classroom projects, and finally, writing the book. There are people to thank all along the way.

As I researched the book forms, the following people shared their knowledge and their collections: Sidney Tai, Yenching Library, Harvard University, Cambridge, MA; Edmund Barry Gaither, Museum of the National Center of Afro-American Artists, Boston, MA; Gretchen Walsh and Augustus Kwaa, African Studies Library, Boston University, Boston, MA; and Elaine Koretsky, Carriage House Papers, Brookline, MA.

As I adapted the material for students, I was given invaluable assistance by all the teachers in my workshops. Their ideas and comments have always been useful and their enthusiasm has been a source of inspiration. The teachers in the Newburyport, Massachusetts Public Schools and their classes who created the student work photographed here deserve special thanks: at the Bresnahan School, Janice Green, Sue LaBay, Maureen Wecal, Lynda Moynahan, Janet Murphy, Nonie Damon, Ann Marie Dean, Alice McLeod, and Judy Fuller; at the Kelley School, Maureen Lee; at the Brown School, Pam Moore, Pam Kent, and Karen Sullivan; and at the Nock Middle School, Nicky Stasewski, Claudia Peresman, and Cliff Smith. Marinel McGrath, Curriculum Coordinator, helped to gather the group of teachers. Mary Bragg, Children's Librarian, and the rest of the staff at the Newburyport Public Library gave the children a forum for exhibiting their work and have helped me in my research over the years.

The book itself began when Helen Moore Sorvillo of Scholastic Professional Books visited my workshop at the 1993 New England Reading Association Conference. I am grateful for her confidence. The book has been enhanced by the photographs of student work by Jim Higgins. Paul Marion gave me a poet's insight into writing haiku and permission to use two of his haiku. Life during the writing process was made easier by Cabot Stains, especially Peter Bunker and Dick Papenfuss, Kathy Charpentier, Brian Cuffe, Nancy Hajeski, and my family. I have been helped by the emotional and practical support of family and friends over the years, especially Lyn Gaylord. I give thanks to them all, and to my husband, Charlie, and children, Brendan and Kendra, whose love is the greatest gift.

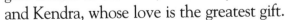

Introduction

About the Book

This book has grown out of work I have been doing in schools for the past five years. I have worked with teachers of all grade levels in public and private schools, as well as at teacher conferences and universities. I have also worked with students, from pre-school through college. Sometimes, the setting is small and intimate. Sometimes, it is a gym with fifty children or seventy-five adults seated at tables. I have learned from them as much as they have learned from me.

The book has two themes: the study of books as an expression of culture and the exploration of the creative possibilities of the book form. Our study takes us around the world and, in many instances, back in time. The inspiration for the projects comes from both contemporary and historical sources.

The reasons for making books are the same in all cultures: the preservation and communication of information, thoughts, and feelings. In some cultures, the oral tradition remains dominant. In others, the written tradition replaces it. The forms of the book vary due to the materials used. The first books were made from available materials: clay, bark, leaves, wood, leather, and cloth. Later, materials were developed specifically for the making of books: papyrus, parchment, and paper. Different materials led to the development of different forms. Cloth and papyrus were rolled into scrolls, strips of wood were tied together, and parchment was folded and sewn.

As we look at traditions from around the world, our opportunities for creativity increase. The books that we normally encounter differ from one another in only two dimensions, the text and the illustrations that are on the pages. We now add a third dimension, in which the books themselves differ, as they are rolled, folded, tied, strung, or sewn together.

The book contains sixteen projects, four from each of four areas of the world: Africa, the Americas, Asia, and Europe. The projects were chosen to represent a variety of cultures, to give a repertoire of book forms to use in other contexts, and to be easily integrated into the classroom with accessible and convenient materials and tools. Within each section, the projects begin with the simplest and progress toward the more difficult.

The projects were all tested by teachers and students in the

Newburyport, Massachusetts Public Schools. I worked with sixteen classes, grades 1 through 6. In most classes, I worked with the students on the construction of the book while the teacher worked with them on the writing and illustration.

Each project, which opens with a photograph of one or more books made by the students, is divided into seven sections.

Materials lists the materials needed. It includes paper in specific sizes, yarn, and beads.

Tools lists the tools needed, such as scissors, markers, and hole punches.

Materials per student allows you to calculate specific amounts needed and is a quick reference when distributing materials.

To Prepare Ahead presents things that need to be done before the book can be made. Students write the texts and plan the layouts prior to making the books. Ideas for content and illustrations are given. In a few projects, there are things that the teacher needs to do before the class makes the book. Sometimes this is for convenience; sometimes, for safety reasons, such as piercing holes in film containers for the Wish Scroll from Ethiopia.

Making the Book has step-by-step instructions for the construction of the book. Because each project is self-contained, instructions are occasionally repeated in more than one book project.

Variations suggests ways to vary the construction and size of the books and gives additional ideas for the content of the books.

Suggested Readings gives a sampling of picture books and folktale collections that can be read as an accompaniment to the projects. Some books have very specific connections and directly echo the theme of the projects. Others are related only in that they are a story from or about that particular culture. A brief description of each book is included, along with publication information.

Materials

*T*he most important material in making the books is paper. There are two weights of paper used, lightweight paper for the pages and heavier paper for the covers and for some pages. Lightweight white paper is available in office supply stores where it is sold in ream packages of 500 sheets for use in copiers. The projects have been designed to use two standard sizes, 8 1/2" x 11" and 11" x 17". For some projects, the paper will need to be cut. For colored paper, 8 1/2" x 11" copier paper and 9" x 12" construction paper are available.

For the heavier weight papers, oak tag and poster board are good choices. I go to a printer and buy what is called "cover stock." It comes in a variety of colors and thicknesses, which are described in pounds. The higher the number of pounds, the heavier the paper. For example, eighty-pound cover is heavier than sixty-pound cover.

You may be able to find a local printer who will donate leftover paper or sell it at a nominal fee. In my experience, it is important to be as clear and concise as possible when dealing with printers. Bring a sample of what you are looking for or happily take whatever they will give you. Frame shops are another source, as they often give or throw away scraps of the colored matboard that is used in framing.

You may also want to start a collection of recycled paper and assorted scraps. Larger pieces can be used for the book itself, smaller pieces for collage. I save wrapping paper, attractive and clean candy wrappers, scraps of art paper and stationery, as well as cardboard used in packaging.

The paper for the books needs to be cut to specific sizes. A paper cutter is helpful. If you get paper from a printer, you might ask him what he would charge to cut the paper to a specific size. It can be a small amount of money and worth the time saved at the paper cutter. The sizes given in the projects are not absolute. I have chosen them to fit with readily available sizes. You can use different sizes, but remember that if the page size changes, the cover size will too. Fold the paper into page size to determine the cover size.

Yarn and ribbon are used in several of the projects. When I give teacher workshops, I try to standardize the materials and use yarn for everything. In many cases, ribbon does look nicer, although it is more expensive. For the sewn books, a heavyweight thread or crochet cotton work well. Embroidery floss is attractive, but the multiple strands can be harder to use. Several of the projects call for pony beads, which are plastic beads with large holes. They are available in craft shops and most reasonably priced in bags of 720.

Tools

Sometimes the most basic tools are hard to come by. Two simple tools that I have often had trouble finding in schools are clean hands and scissors that cut well. It's worth trying for both. Holes are made with hole punches or the pointy end of a pair of scissors or with a nail and hammer and a piece of wood or heavy cardboard to protect the table. Blunt needles with large eyes are used for the sewn books. Because the holes are made first, the needles do not need to be sharp. I use tapestry needles made of steel, but they are also available in plastic. For the writing and illustration of the book, markers or colored pencils are used. Because the pages are small, fine markers or colored pencils are best for all grade levels.

I use glue sticks for all my workshops and recommend them highly. My favorite kind is UHU by FaberCastell, which sticks well and doesn't dry too quickly. It goes on purple so you can see where the glue is and dries clear. The bigger sizes are more economical if you are vigilant about replacing the covers at the end of the project. Some office supply stores and catalogs sell them in quantity for reasonable prices. I find the containers of wet glue that roll on to be more difficult to use. Rubber cement is a no-no. The fumes are unsafe and it yellows with age. Any project with gluing also needs scrap paper. I use pages from old telephone books when I go to schools and junk mail when I'm at home.

Before I discovered the advantages of glue sticks, I used homemade cooked flour paste and a brush. In the following recipe, I usually make it with one part equaling 1/2 cup. Wallpaper paste or school paste thinned with just enough water to be brushed are also possibilities.

Cooked Flour Paste

1 part flour   1 part cold water   2 parts boiling water

Put the flour in a pan or a double boiler. Add the cold water gradually, stirring until all lumps are removed. A whisk works well. Slowly add the boiling water and cook the mixture 3-4 minutes, stirring constantly. Cover it and let it cool. If you wish, add a drop or two of oil of cloves, which is available in pharmacies, for a preservative and stir.

If you use a microwave, you only have to cook the mixture 1-2 minutes and you don't need to stir. It will expand as it cooks so leave room in the cooking container. Store the unused paste in a covered container in the refrigerator, where it will keep for about two weeks.

Basic Techniques

The basic techniques of constructing and writing in the book are explained here, as a supplement to the information in the project sections.

Folding

Folding is an important element in making books. Neat folds make neat books. All the folding in the projects involves folding the paper in half. In some instances, the halves are folded in half again. The directions are given for those who are right-handed. Reverse the hands if you are left-handed.

Line up Corners A and B.

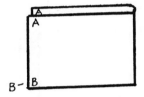

With the corners lined up, use your left hand to hold the paper in place.

Starting at Corner A, run the thumb of your right hand along the top of the paper. When you get to Corner C, press down with your thumb to flatten the paper and start the fold. Then, run your thumb down the side to Corner D to make the entire fold. To make a sharper crease, go back over the fold with the flat part of your fingernail.

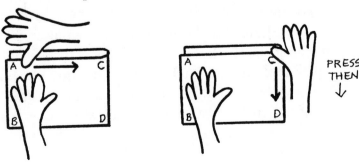

Gluing

As I said in the Materials section, glue stick is my preference. However, the method of application is always the same, whatever you use. The glue is put on the smaller of the two pieces that are being attached in a thin coat that covers the entire surface. Scrap paper is always used. In covering the entire surface, you need to go over the edges. If you get glue on the table, you risk having your book get stuck to the table.

Place the paper to be glued on scrap paper. Cover the entire surface with a thin coat of glue or paste. Start in the middle and work toward the edges. Go over the edges and onto the scrap paper. If you want glue on only a part of a larger piece of paper, you will need 2 pieces of scrap paper. Place the book paper on one sheet of scrap paper. Place the second sheet of scrap paper on the book paper, covering everything but the part on which you want to have glue.

 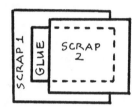

After the paper is covered with glue, carefully position it on the other piece of paper. When it is in the proper place, smooth over it with your hand to adhere. If you make a mistake and position the glued piece improperly, you can often correct it if you work quickly before the glue has dried and you have pressed to adhere. Discard the scrap paper so that you don't use it again by mistake. When any kind of wet paste is used, the moisture will cause the paper to buckle. To alleviate the problem, the books should be wrapped in waxed paper and pressed flat under heavy books or other weights until dry.

Making Holes

A hole punch is used for several of the projects. If you don't have a hole punch, the pointy end of a scissor can be poked through the paper and twisted to make a hole. The holes made by the punch will look neater.

In some projects, the holes are made by hitting a nail or an awl. An awl or ice pick and hammer make holes more quickly, but hitting a nail with a block of wood is safer. The nail isn't as sharp as the awl or ice pick. If you hit your fingers by mistake, the block of wood is less painful than a hammer. I use an awl and hammer when I am making the holes and have students use a nail and a block of wood. An extra piece of wood is always needed to place underneath to protect the table.

Tying Knots

Tying knots can be a challenge. I have used projects with knots from first grade up but wait until third grade for the large groups of fifty students. And then, I meet the occasional fifth grader who says, "I can't tie."

All of the knots used are double knots. The simplest ones are just two knots, tied one after the other. I tell students to begin as if they are tying their shoes. After they make the first knot, they make a second knot instead of the bow they would make for their shoes.

In a few of the projects, beads are tied onto a cord. This is done by stringing the cord through the bead first (a). One knot is tied (b) and tightened around the bead (c). The bead is inside the knot. A second knot is then tied to secure it (d). It helps to tug on the bead at the end to tighten the knot.

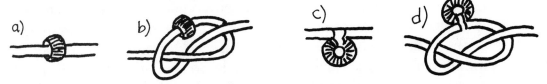

Square knots, which are more secure, are a kind of double knot. They are more complicated, because it matters which hand is holding which cord. You may remember square knots from Girl or Boy Scouts, "right over left, left over right." They are used for the two sewn bindings, The Book of Haiku and the Medieval Book. I usually do these sewn bindings in small groups and sometimes end up tying the knots for the students.

Each hand holds one end of the cord. The cord that is in your right hand goes on top of the cord that is in your left hand (right over left). For the second knot, the cord that is in your left hand goes on top of the cord that is in your right hand (left over right). Pull to tighten.

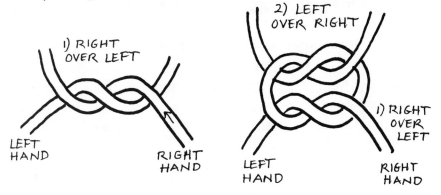

Writing the Texts

Writing for a book is different from writing a composition because there are limitations to the size and number of the pages. If the students do their drafts on paper the same size as the pages in the book, it will make for a smoother transition to the finished book.

Writing in the book itself has its own set of problems. Because the paper is not lined, keeping the writing straight can be difficult. For some of the projects, line guides have been included. These can be copied and cut out. They are placed under the page of the book. The students write the text using the lines as they show through the page or trace the lines in pencil and write the text later. If they have trouble seeing the lines, they can try holding the paper and the guide against a window, where the light makes the lines easier to see. If the page slips off the line guide, masking tape can be used to hold them together. Be sure to pull off the masking tape gently.

The other difficulty is writing without mistakes. Some books are made of separate pages that are bound together at the end. These are relatively easy to deal with, as a page with an error can be discarded and redone. Other books are made from one piece of paper and represent a challenge. Being careful is not always enough. The writing can be done in pencil, so that errors can be erased. The writing can be done first in pencil, checked carefully, then traced over with thin black marker. The writing can be done in fine black marker or pen and mistakes can be covered with correction fluid. Test the fluid with the marker on a piece of scrap paper before using it in the book. It will sometimes cause the marker to bleed. If, after all this, the books have spelling errors, remember that these are handmade books. Even the beautiful illuminated manuscripts made by medieval monks had mistakes.

Illustrations

The illustrations in the projects are either drawings or cut paper collage. There are other possibilities as well. I reluctantly, because of cost, began collecting rubber stamps and have found them very useful. I use the standard color stamp pads from office supply stores or have the students color the stamps with markers. I have made stencils on a variety of subjects, such as sea life, by tracing pictures from books, transferring the image to poster board, covering it with clear contact paper for longevity, and cutting out the stencil. Pictures can be cut from magazines. Printmaking, with potatoes or styrofoam trays from grocery stores, is messier, but effective. Because most children prefer doing the illustrations to writing, I usually save them for last.

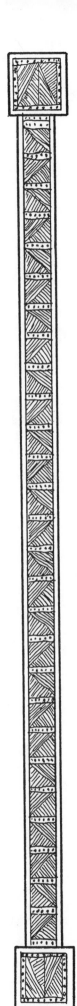

Africa

Historical Overview,
page 21

Projects

Africa has a rich history of both written and oral traditions. One of the earliest book forms, the papyrus scroll, came from ancient Egypt. Christianity in the fourth century and Islam in the seventh century brought additional influences. Africa's oral tradition is often enhanced and aided by a variety of storytelling devices and memory aids on cloth, wood, and with beads.

The scrolls of ancient Egypt and Nubia were made of papyrus, a plant that grows along the Nile. The stems were cut into thin strips. The strips were laid on top of each other in two layers, one horizontally and one vertically. They were then pressed until they meshed together to form a paper-like substance. The papyrus pieces were usually made in small sections that were glued together and rolled to form a scroll. The scroll was used for all manner of government and business records, as well as religious writings, literature, and science books. One of the most common books was The Book of the Dead, which contained descriptions of the afterlife and were buried with the dead. The writing, done with a reed and ink made from carbon, was called hieroglyphics, or picture writing. Papyrus scrolls were in use from about 3000 B.C. until the 4th century A.D. Their influence was widespread in the ancient world, including classical Greece and Rome.

Perhaps the most well-known Christian group in Africa were the Copts of Egypt, who converted to Christianity in the second century. Already well versed in the arts of writing and bookbinding, they made books of papyrus and leather and bound them in the codex form of folded sheets sewn together along the fold. Thick covers of pressed papyrus, rather like heavy cardboard, were covered with leather and decorated. Their particular way of sewing the book together, with the thread exposed along the spine, is still used today by bookbinders and called the Coptic binding. Despite the Arab conquest of Egypt in 641, the Copts continued to speak their own language until the thirteenth century, and it remained the liturgical language into the seventeenth century.

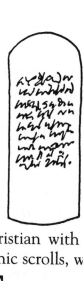

Islam was the other major influence on book production in Africa. Scrolls were widely used in all of Islamic Africa from the seventh century. In West Africa, the Koran is taught to students in Arabic by means of wooden boards. Some boards have the texts written on them. Others are for students to practice writing. The writing is done with charcoal and washed clean after using. The boards start out a light color and darken with use. Ethiopia, primarily Christian with Islamic, Jewish, and pagan influences, developed talismanic scrolls, which were worn as protection and prayer.

There is a strong storytelling tradition in Africa on cloth. The court of Dahomey in Benin, western Africa, had appliqué cloths made to commemorate their lives and important events. In Ghana, adinkra cloths are made by printing fabric with stamps carved from gourds. The patterns are chosen from a set of symbols, each with its own special meaning. The cloths were originally made as mourning cloths, but have expanded to other uses.

Printed cloths, which were worn, played an important part in the independence movements in Africa in the 1960's. They promoted national identity, democracy, and literacy. They are still made today with public health and political messages.

There are other examples of communication devices from different parts of Africa. Young Zulu women send messages to their boyfriends and husbands through pieces of handmade beadwork. In Zaire, the Luba make Lukasa, decorated boards which pass on the mythology and morals of the secret society to initiates.

Name Scroll
Egypt

This project uses the scroll from Egypt to explore the development of our alphabet from the pictographic writing of Egyptian hieroglyphs to the Roman letters that we use today. The earliest writing was in the form of picture symbols, or pictographs. As time went on, the pictures came to represent sounds. Because they were time consuming to draw, the pictures slowly changed into abstract symbols representing sounds, that is, an alphabet.

In the name scroll, the students create their own picture-sound alphabets. Each letter of their names is represented by a picture of something that starts with that letter. The scrolls illustrated here were made by first graders Heather and Alex. The assembly was done in small groups, as adult assistance was often needed.

Materials:

Cardboard tubes, 2 1/4" high, Toilet paper tubes cut in half, or paper towel tubes cut with scissors. The tubes will squish down during cutting, but bounce back to their original shape.

Lightweight paper, 2 1/4" x 28": Adding machine tape

Yarn, 12" length

Tools:

Scissors

Glue stick and scrap paper

Stapler (optional)

Hole punch

Markers, crayons, or colored pencils

Materials per student:

1 tube 2 1/4" high

1 strip of paper 2 1/4" x 28"

1 piece yarn, 12" long

To Prepare Ahead

1. Discuss development of our alphabet. Have the students collect pictures that start with the letters of the alphabet. Look at alphabet books. Plan the pictures that students will use to write their names. Do a rough draft of the pictures if desired.

2. Optional: To move the project more quickly, you may want to attach the paper to the tubes for the students. Wrap the paper around the tube and staple at the top and the bottom. You will then skip Steps 1 and 3.

Development of Our Alphabet

from Egyptian Hieroglyphs

EGYPTIAN HIEROGLYPH →	TRANSITIONAL STAGES →	ROMAN ALPHABET
OX		→ A
HOUSE		→ B
DOOR		→ D
WATER		→ M
FISH		→ N
EYE		→ O
MOUTH		→ R
TOOTH		→ S

Making the Book

1. Draw a line 6" from the edge of the paper. If the paper starts to curl up, tape it to the desk with masking tape or weight it down with a ruler or other object.

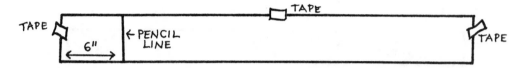

2. Write name with pictures, starting about 1" to the right of the line.

3. To attach the paper to the roll:

a. Apply glue to the paper from the edge up to the line. Use scrap paper and go over the edges onto the scrap paper. Masking tape will be helpful again if the paper begins to curl.

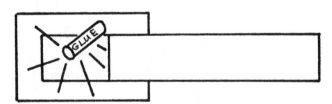

b. Place the tube on the end of the paper with the glue. Make sure that the sides of the paper line up with the edges of the tube as evenly as possible. Roll the tube slowly toward you to wrap the paper around the tube and press to stick.

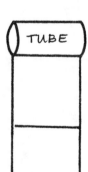
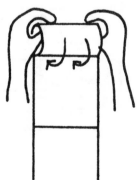

4. Leave about 3" blank paper beyond the name pictures. Trim off any excess paper.

5. Fold the edge over twice. Each folded section should be about 3/4".

6. Punch a hole through the center of the folded sections.

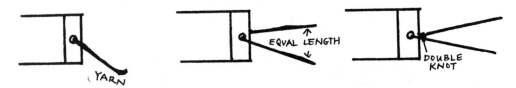

7. Thread the yarn through the hole. Pull the yarn through until you have two strands of equal length. Tie a double knot against the end of the paper.

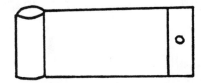

8. Roll up the scroll. Wrap one end of yarn around the scroll to the right and the other end around to the left. Halfway around the scroll, tie the two strands in a double knot. You have now made a loop of yarn that can be placed around the scroll to hold it closed and lifted off to open it.

Variations

Instead of drawing pictures, cut them from magazines and paste them on the scroll. Use colored paper for the scroll.

Use the name scroll as a starting point for a discussion of the meaning of names. Books for new parents to choose names are a good source of information. Have the students find out why their parents chose their particular names.

Vary the size and the materials. Mount the paper on paper towel rolls or wooden dowels. Use light-colored cloth or wallpaper for the scroll. Make a tie with ribbons.

Make a large class scroll. Stores that sell carpets or fabrics can be a source for long sturdy cardboard tubes. Rolls of white paper, 12", 24", and 36" wide, are available in some art shops. Local newspapers can be a source of newsprint rolls. Have each student write his or her name in pictures in a vertical column. Have each student draw a picture of himself. If paper is large enough, have each student lay down and trace the outline of her body and fill it in.

Suggested Readings

The Day of Ahmed's Secret, Florence Parry Heide and Judith Heide Gilliland. New York: Lothrop, Lee, and Shepard, 1990. Ahmed, a young boy in contemporary Egypt, spends his days delivering water. The sights and sounds of Cairo are vividly described, and at the end of the day, he reveals his secret: he has learned to write his name.

The Egyptian Cinderella, Shirley Climo. New York: Crowell, 1989. Set in Egypt in the sixth century B.C., this Cinderella is Rhodopes, a slave girl who is chosen by the pharaoh to be queen.

How Djadja-Em-Ankh Saved the Day: A Tale from Ancient Egypt, Lise Manniche. New York: Thomas Y. Crowell Company, 1976. This story of King Seneferu and the magician Djadja-Em-Ankh was translated from a scroll that was written more than 2,500 years ago in Egypt. The accordion fold book has the story on one side and historical information on the other.

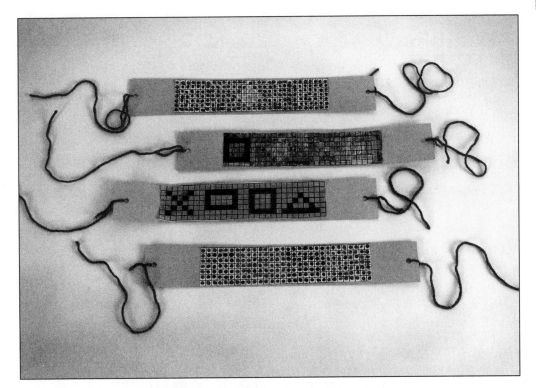

Zulu Beadwork
South Africa

Zulu girls and women make beadwork articles for their boyfriends and husbands. Small colored glass seed beads are sewn into neckbands or rectangular pendants. The beadwork is more than just ornament; it sends a message. Colors and shapes stand for particular emotions and thoughts. They can express positive emotions of love and happiness, but also jealousy and loneliness if separated. Small rectangular pieces of beadwork mounted on large safety pins are also made for sale and called Zulu Love Tokens. Beadwork is also made in other parts of Africa. The Samburu of Kenya and the Maasai of Kenya and Tanzania make beadwork that communicates information about a person's status, whether it be unmarried woman or man, mother, elder, or priest. The neckbands illustrated here were made by third graders. They created their own language of shape and color. After brainstorming as a class, each student assigned his or her own meanings. They enjoyed choosing the feelings to match the symbols and expressing themselves through color and shape. However, they found the actual making of the neckband to be tedious. Therefore, on page 32 I have added directions for making a smaller pendant.

Materials:

Photocopies of grid

Heavy paper or oak tag, 2" x 10"

Yarn in 20" lengths

Pony beads (optional)

Tools:

Markers, colored pencils, or crayons

Scissors

Hole punch

Glue stick and scrap paper

Materials per student:

Photocopy of grid

Strip of heavy paper or oak tag, 2" x 10"

2 pieces of yarn, 20" long

4 pony beads (optional)

To Prepare Ahead

Assign meanings to the colors and shapes. Students may use the colors and shapes listed with the grid or come up with their own. A sample of assigned meanings from the students' work: Blue-surprised, Red-dissapointed, Yellow-sad, Black-confused, Green-glad, X-not, Triangle-tears, Diamond-laughter, Square-smile, Zigzag Line-frown. Copy extra grids if students wish to try out different ideas. There will be a background color and one or more shapes in different colors. The shapes may be centered on the grid or placed assymetrically. Centering is more difficult.

Grid for Beadwork

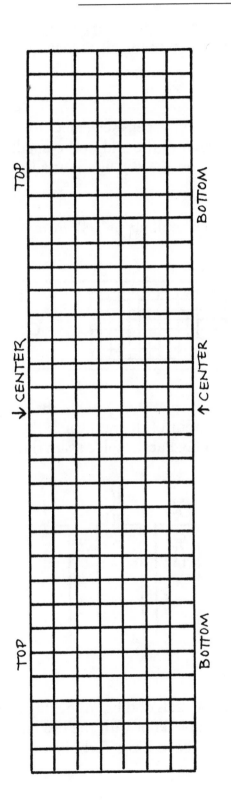

Colors

Blue _____

Red _____

Yellow _____

Black _____

Green _____

Shapes

X _____

Triangle _____

Diamond _____

Square _____

Zigzag line _____

Making the Book

1. Color in the grid. The squares may be completely colored in, or for a more beaded look, a dot can be drawn to fill each square.

2. Cut out the grid.

3. Glue the grid to the strip of construction paper. Remember to cover the entire surface and use scrap paper . Center the grid in the middle of the strip. There will be a narrow border on the top and bottom and a wider border on each side.

4. Punch a hole at each end of the neckband, about 1/4" in from the edges and centered from top to bottom.

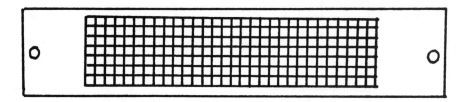

5. Fold one piece of yarn in half. Put the loop at the center of the folded yarn through the hole, starting from the front of the neckband. Pull the loop from the back of the hole and open it up. Put the folded yarn through the loop and pull to tighten.

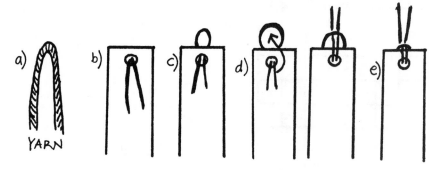

6. Repeat with the second piece of yarn.

7. Optional: Tie the four pony beads to the ends of the yarn by threading the yarn through the bead and tying a double knot with the bead inside the knot. A diagram can be found on page 17 in Basic Techniques.

Pendant

The materials are the same as for the neckband, except

Heavy paper or oak tag, 2" x 3 1/2"

Yarn or cord in 36" lengths

Photocopies of small grid

Materials per student:

Photocopy of small grid

1 piece heavy paper or oak tag, 2" x 3 1/2"

1 piece of yarn, 36" long

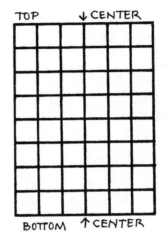

1. Color and cut out the small grid.

2. Fold a 1" tab on the long side of the heavy paper to form a rectangle that is 2" x 2 1/2".

3. Hold the grid vertically. Glue it onto the heavy paper, centering it.

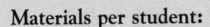

4. Tie the two ends of a 36" length of yarn together with a double knot. Put glue on the back side of the tab. Place the yarn in the fold with the knot in the center of the fold. Rub the tab to adhere.

DOUBLE KNOT

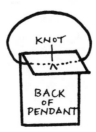

KNOT

BACK OF PENDANT

Variations

Use 1/4" round color coding labels available in office supply stores for the beads. They are self-adhesive and will fit into the grid. They are available in yellow, red, green, and blue. I've also tried gluing on colored paper circles made with a hole punch, which is tedious.

For older students, use 1/8" graph paper and fine markers for a more detailed look.

Make a pendant by gluing beads onto a piece of cardboard. Use white tacky glue and beads large enough to handle easily.

Make necklaces or pendants for Mother's or Father's Day gifts or other occasions. Write the meaning of the colors and shapes on the back so that the recipient can decode the message.

Suggested Reading

Shaka, King of the Zulus, Diane Stanley and Peter Vennema. New York: Morrow Jr. Books, 1988. This is the story of Shaka and his journey from outcast to king and fierce and innovative war leader. Drawings of beadwork run throughout the book as border elements and complement the rich illustrations.

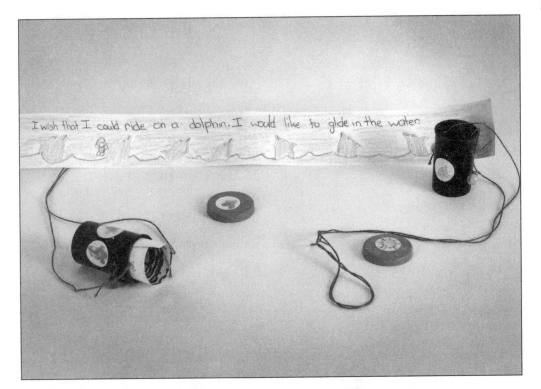

I wish that I could ride on a dolphin. I would like to glide in the water.

Wish Scroll
Ethiopia

Small scrolls of vellum (specially treated animal hide), were, and still are, made in Ethiopia. They are placed in cases of metal or leather and worn, either tied to a belt or hung around the neck. The scrolls are talismans, containing prayers for personal protection and cures for the sick. While most other books are used to disseminate and share information, these books are private and made for a single individual.

This project is designed to use a plastic film container as the case for the scroll. A wish or dream is written on a strip of paper, which is then rolled up and placed in a case that can be worn around the neck. The scrolls can be shared or kept private.

The scrolls in the photograph were done by third grade students. I have used this lesson successfully with all grade levels. Students all seem to like the idea of writing and wearing their own wishes.

Materials:

Strips of paper, 1 3/4" x 17"

Plastic 35 mm film containers

Cord, crochet cotton, (thin and easy to thread through hole), narrow ribbon or string in 40" lengths

Pony beads (plastic beads with large holes)

White circle labels, 3/4" diameter

Tools:

Awl, ice pick, or nail

Markers and/or colored pencils

Materials per student:

1 strip of paper, 1 3/4" x 17"

1 film container with lid

1 length of cord, 40" long

2 pony beads

3 white circle labels

To Prepare Ahead

1. Pierce two holes in each film container with an awl, an ice pick, or a nail. Awls and ice picks work better as the handles give you better leverage and they have a longer shaft. The holes should be on opposite sides of the container about 3/8" down from the top. It is easiest to pierce both holes at the same time. Push in the tool you are using as far as you can to get the largest hole possible.

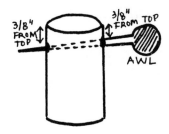

An alternative is to make a hole on each side by poking and twisting the point of small sharp scissors, such as embroidery scissors.

2. Prepare drafts of text. Possible starting points: I wish. . ., My dream is. . ., May there be. . ., etc. The wishes can be imaginary: "I wish I could sail in a sea of stars"; for personal gratification: "I wish I had a new computer game"; or for the world: "May there be peace in the world and in our hearts." Ideas for illustrations can be worked on now or later.

Making the Book

1. Write the wish on a strip of paper. The paper can be held either vertically (more traditional) or horizontally. Add illustrations or borders if desired.

2. To tie the bead to one end of the string, with the bead inside the knot:
  a. Put the string through the hole in one bead.
  b. Tie a knot at one end of the string.
  c. Tighten the knot around the bead.
  d. Tie a second knot to secure it. Tug on the bead to tighten the knot.

3. Take the lid off the container. Push the end of the string without the bead through a hole in the container. It will be easier to get the string through the hole if you start with the bigger hole, that is, the one you pierced first. Go through the middle of the container and out the hole on the other side.

4. Put the end of the string through the hole in the other bead. Tie a double knot at the end of the string with the bead inside the knot. Tug on the bead to tighten the knot.

5. Pull up the string from the middle of the container until the beads touch the sides.

6. Decorate circle labels with stars, dots, lines, or something to match the illustrations on the scrolls.

7. Place labels on the container, one on the lid and one on each side.

8. Roll up the scroll, place it in its case, and close the lid.

Variations

Celebrate holidays with gift scrolls. Make them for Christmas, Mother's Day, Father's Day, or birthdays.

Use when studying recycling and the environment or for Earth Day. Use only recycled materials. Try grocery bags for the paper, used ribbon or string, and old buttons instead of the beads. Write a wish for the earth.

Work with a local hospital and make get-well scrolls for the patients. One of the original purposes of the scrolls is writing out cures.

Write a scroll with "I wish I were _____ because. . ." If you are studying history, the student decides which historical person he or she would like to be. Or choose which kind of animal, sea creature, dinosaur, character in a book, etc.

Suggested Readings

The Miracle Child: A Story from Ethiopia, Elizabeth Laird with Abba Aregawi Wolde Gabriel. Holt, Rinehart and Winston. New York: 1985. Ethiopia is one of the oldest Christian countries in the world. This story of the famous Ethiopian saint, St. Tekla Haymanot, is illustrated with pictures from an eighteenth-century manuscript.

The Fire on the Mountain and Other Ethiopian Stories, Harold Courlander and Wolf Leslau. Henry Holt and Company. New York: 1950. This collection of stories, excellent for reading aloud, tells stories about men and animals and their wisdom and folly and the pursuit of justice. The book contains notes on the backgrounds of the stories.

Adinkra Cloth
Ghana

Adinkra cloths are made in Ghana. First made as mourning cloths, they came to be used for other occasions as well. Kings and rich people commissioned cloths to speak of their power. People embarking on a new venture, such as starting a business, might commission a cloth. Most cloths are printed, although some are appliquéd. The stamps for printing are cut from a gourd. The black dye is a mixture made from the boiled bark of the badie tree and an iron-rich stone. The dye is called adinkra, which means "farewell." The symbols used in printing have a long tradition and deep significance. Through the symbols, each cloth communicates information about the owner, living or dead. The symbols are so much a part of Ghanian culture that they are often used by the government and clergy. The logo of the Standards Board in Ghana is the measuring rod, which stands for excellence and intolerance of imperfection.

The construction paper cloths shown here were made by fourth graders. Most used the patterns provided. Some had difficulty doing precise cutting. This is one place where good scissors are a real plus. The students made cloths for parents, grandparents, friends, historical figures, and themselves.

Materials:

9" x 12" sheets of colored construction paper

Black paper, construction or other, in 4" squares

Yarn in 12" lengths

Patterns for symbols glued onto poster board

Tools:

Pencil for tracing

Scissors

Glue stick and scrap paper

Stapler

Paper clips

White tacky glue (optional)

Materials per student:

1 sheet of 9" x 12" construction paper

6 pieces of black paper, 4" square

To Prepare Ahead

1. Make the patterns for the symbols. Photocopy the patterns on page 42. Glue them onto a sheet of poster board or light cardboard. If you plan to do this project more than once, cover the poster board with clear contact paper for greater longevity. Cut out the patterns. It can be difficult to maneuver the scissors into some of the small spaces. If you are comfortable using an X-acto knife or razor blade, you may find it easier. The project will go more quickly if there are several sets of patterns for the class to use.

2. Plan the adinkra cloths. Students choose a person, living or dead, real or imaginary, for whom the cloth will be made. They then choose symbols to represent the person. The symbols and their meanings are illustrated on page 43. There are patterns to trace for nine symbols. The others can be drawn or enlarged and traced. Students can also create their own symbols. Six symbols will be used for each cloth. They can all be different or there can be some repetition. Students also choose the color of the construction paper "cloth." For mourning cloths, brown is the traditional color.

Making the Book

1. To cut six symbols from the black paper squares:

    a. Use the patterns on the next page. Fold the black paper in half. Place the pattern on the paper with the edges of the pattern marked "fold" along the folded side of the paper. Use paper clips to hold the pattern in place. Trace the outline with a pencil. Keep the paper folded and cut along the line. Do not cut the fold. Open and smooth out the symbol.

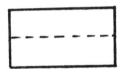

    b. Use symbols on page 43 as a guide and draw and cut out your own.

2. Fold the sheet of construction paper in half vertically.

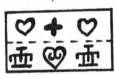

3. The fold divides the paper into two sections. Glue the symbols to the paper in two rows. When applying the glue, use scrap paper and cover the entire surface of the back of each symbol.

4. To attach the yarn to the paper with two or three strands along the top edge, the bottom edge, and the center fold:

    a. With a stapler: It is helpful to work in pairs. One student holds the yarn while the other staples it to the paper. It can be difficult to catch all the strands of yarn within the staple.

    b. With glue stick or white glue: Run glue stick or white tacky glue along the center fold to form a line of glue. Place the yarn on the line of glue and press. A partner may be helpful again here, one to hold the yarn and one to press. Repeat with the top and bottom edges.

Patterns for Adinkra Symbols

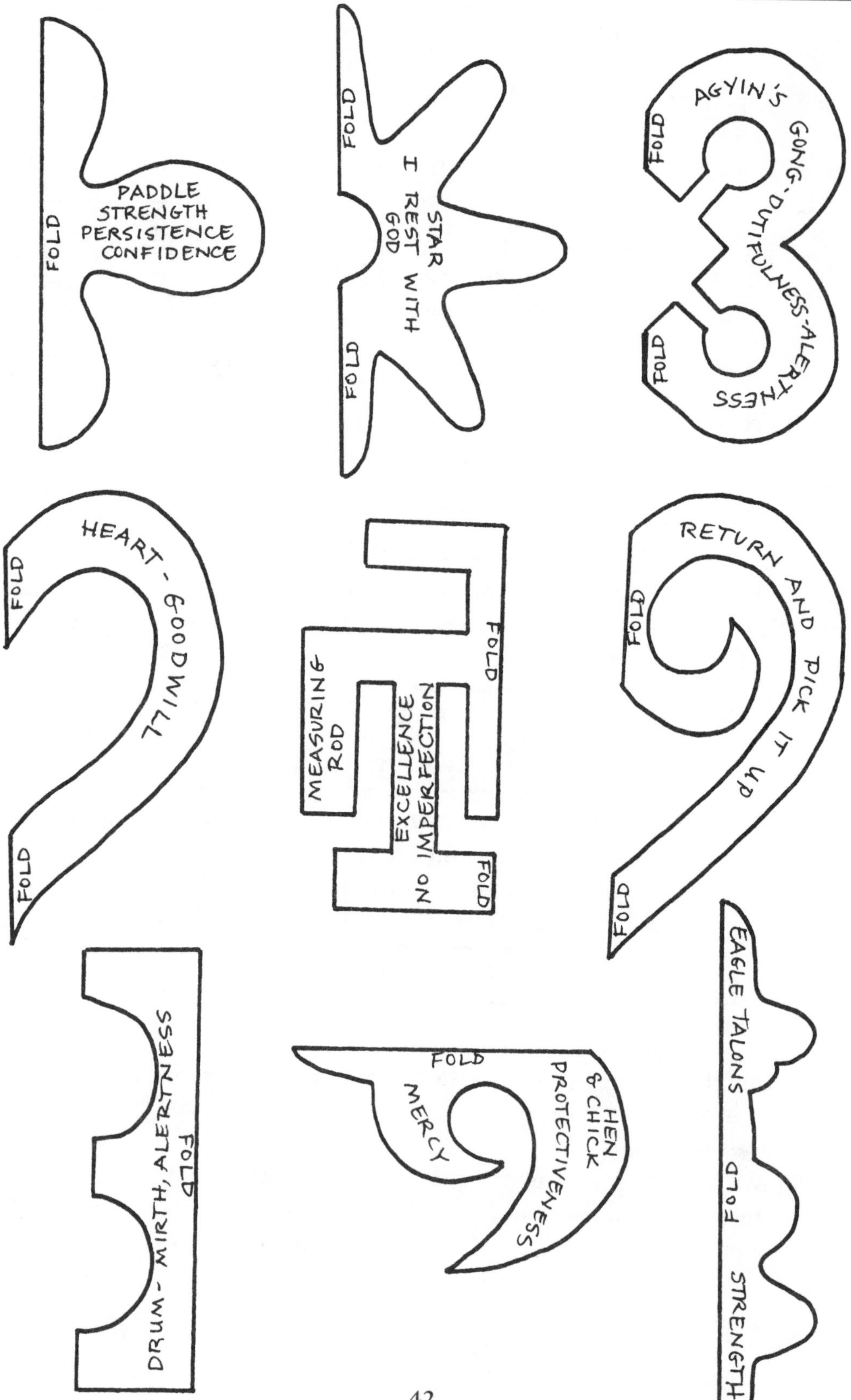

PADDLE
STRENGTH
PERSISTENCE
CONFIDENCE

FOLD

STAR
I REST WITH GOD

FOLD

FOLD

AGYIN'S GONG - DUTIFULNESS - ALERTNESS

FOLD

FOLD

HEART - GOODWILL

FOLD

FOLD

MEASURING ROD

EXCELLENCE

NO IMPERFECTION

FOLD

FOLD

RETURN AND PICK IT UP

FOLD

FOLD

DRUM - MIRTH, ALERTNESS

FOLD

MERCY

FOLD

HEN & CHICK PROTECTIVENESS

EAGLE TALONS

FOLD

STRENGTH

Adinkra Symbols

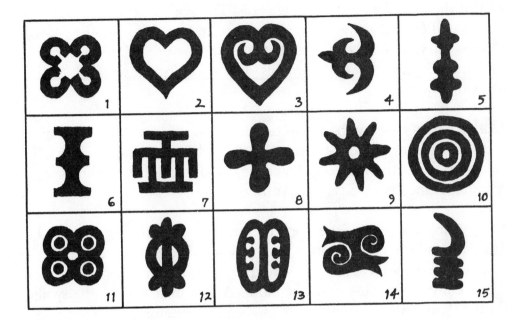

1. **Agyinda wuru**, Agyin's gong. Agyin was a faithful servant to King of Asante. Symbol of alertness and dutifulness.

2. **Akoma**, heart. Symbol of goodwill, patience, fondness, faithfulness.

3. **Sankofa**, "Return and pick it up." Learn from or build on the past. Pick up what's good in the past to bring to the future.

4. **Akoko nan tia ne ba a enkum no**, "If a hen steps on its chick, the chick does not die." Symbol of mercy, protectiveness, discipline with patience.

5. **Okodee mmowere**, eagle's talons. Symbol of strength.

6. **Donno ntoasa**, drum. Symbol of merriment, alertness, skill with hands.

7. **Hwemudua**, measuring rod. Symbol of excellence, intolerance of imperfection.

8. **Tabono**, paddle for canoe. Symbol of strength, confidence, persistence.

9. **Nsoromma**, star. "Like the star, the child of the Supreme Being, I rest with God and so I do not depend on myself."

10. **Adinkrahene**, king of the adinkra designs. Symbol of greatness, prudence, firmness, and magnamity.

11. **Ntesie or Matie masie**, "What I hear, I keep." Symbol of wisdom, knowledge, prudence.

12. **Wawa aba**, seeds of owawa tree. Symbol of hardiness; sticks to goals.

13. **Ese ne tekrema**, teeth and tongue. Symbol of friendliness and interdependence.

14. **Kwatakye atiko**, back of Kwatakye's head. Special hairstyle of captain of old Asante. Symbol of bravery and valor.

15. **Akoben**, war horn. Symbol of readiness to be called to arms.

Variations

Have the class design its own symbols. The symbols on the cloth represent qualities and values that are important to the people of Ghana. Discuss the values and qualities that are important to the class and its culture and design appropriate symbols. The students can work in groups or individually.

Make a class cloth with one section for each student. Mount individual sections on a large piece of paper or bulletin board. Make a large cloth to celebrate the birth of famous Americans, such as Martin Luther King, Jr., Abraham Lincoln, or Susan B. Anthony.

For younger students, use cookie cutters as patterns for the symbols. Trace around the cookie cutter with a pencil directly on the "cloth" and color in the shapes. Or, trace around the cookie cutter on black or colored paper, cut out, and glue onto the cloth. Assign meanings to the symbols. Rather than using yarn, glue strips of colored paper for the borders or draw lines with a crayon or marker.

Make a printed cloth. Cut symbols from slices of potatoes or styrofoam trays. Brush tempera or acrylic paint onto each shape and press it on the cloth. Try it with pieces of cloth rather than paper.

Suggested Readings

Anansi the Spider: A Tale from the Ashanti, adapted and illustrated by Gerald McDermott. New York: Holt, Rinehart and Winston, 1972. A graphically stunning retelling of the story of Anansi and his six sons who work together to save their father when he is in danger. Of interest to this project is the fact that the sons all have the same legs and heads and are distinguished from one another by the symbols that make up their bodies.

The Hat-Shaking Dance and Other Ashanti Tales from Ghana, Harold Courlander with Albert Kofi Prempeh. New York: Harcourt, Brace & World, Inc., 1957. Twenty-one Ashanti tales from Ghana, excellent for reading aloud, are featured in this book. Many are about Anansi, the spider, including "All Stories Are Anansi's."

The Americas

Historical Overview,
page 47

Projects

The history of the book in the Americas can be divided into two broad categories: books by the indigenous peoples and books brought by the Europeans.

The most developed indigenous book form was the codex of the Mayans and Aztecs of Mexico and Central America. These accordion books were made of deerskin or a paper made from the inner bark of the fig tree, which was boiled and then pounded until it meshed together. The folded books, usually with wooden covers, were used for ritual calendars, tribute lists, genealogies, and historical chronicles. Glyphs, or small pictures, were the writing, with the pictures representing sounds as well as specific objects. Most of the codices were destroyed by the Spanish, with less than 20 pre-Conquest books extant. The oldest, the Dresden Codex, dates from the twelfth century.

In South America, the Inca of Peru made *quipu*, which were knotted strings called "remembering strings." Quipu were an important tool in the Inca empire, which stretched from Ecuador to Chile. There were two types: those used for accounting, in which the knots recorded the production and distribution of crops, and other goods, as well as population counts, and those in which the knots represented words.

The native North American book traditions include a variety of pictographic work. The Ojibwa in Minnesota made birch bark scrolls to preserve the knowledge needed for the *Midewiwin*, or Medicine Dance. The Dakota made "winter counts," which recorded their history on buffalo hides. Other Plains Indians also preserved the memory of important events on buffalo hides. The Eastern Woodland Indians made wampum belts of shell beads. The patterns and colors transmitted messages and recorded important events, such as treaties. After the coming of the white people, many imprisoned Indians made drawings in ledgers and on pieces of muslin cloth. These are now called Ledger Art.

The Europeans brought with them their tradition of books and binding. Printing was already well established in Europe, and printing presses made their way to the New World. In 1539, the first printer came from Spain to Mexico, where most of the books were religious texts in the native languages that were needed by the missionaries. Printing came to New England in 1638 in conjunction with the beginning of Harvard College, eighteen years after the arrival of the Pilgrims. The important books in colonial times were the Bible, books of psalms and sermons, and yearly almanacs, which were considered necessities and hung by a string near the door. The most famous almanac is *Poor Richard's Almanac* by Benjamin Franklin, who was then known as a printer. When he decided to write as well as print the almanac to save the author's fee, he used a pseudonym. Students in colonial times learned from hornbooks, paddle-shaped pieces of wood with instructional papers protected by a layer of horn.

As technology hastened the printing process and developed ways of making paper from wood pulp, books became more widespread. The book in America since the coming of the Europeans is distinguished more by the development of the content than the form. Our projects will take us from the Aztecs and Mayans of Mexico and Central America to contemporary popular culture in the United States.

Winter Count
Dakota Indians, North America

The Dakota counted years by winters and chronicled their history in Winter Counts. While it is called a count, the Dakota did not number the winters or years, but rather gave them names. For example, the winter of 1883-84 was distinguished by a great meteor shower and was called "plenty-stars winter." Each winter a picture was drawn on a buffalo skin to represent the significant event of the year. An example from the Yanktonnai tribe of Montana began in 1800-01 with three rows of ten vertical lines to represent thirty Dakotas 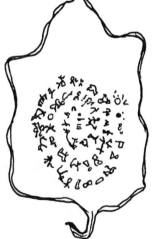 killed by Crow. The chronicle begins at the center and follows a spiral shape. The next-to-the-last symbol, a black circle, stands for a total eclipse of the sun in 1869-70.

This project was done by third graders, using grocery bags. Some students got very involved in making the bags resemble animal skin. Others were more interested in their drawings. It is best to use black marker or crayon, especially if the counts are going to be displayed. Some counts with wonderful drawings in pencil were almost impossible to "read."

Materials:

Brown grocery bags

Tools:

Brown or black crayons, paper wrapping removed

Black markers or crayons

Materials per student:

1 brown grocery bag

To Prepare Ahead

Plan the winter count. Students can make winter counts of their own lives. They can represent each year with a picture, or go day by day or week by week. While the yearly count is traditional, a daily count over several weeks gives a better feeling for the process, which occurred over time. The annual marking of the hide must have been a significant event in itself.

The following pictures illustrate four days in winter.
1. We built a snowman.
2. We went sledding.
3. I went to the library.
4. It was a sunny, warm day.

  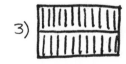 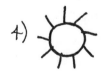

Making the Book

1. Tear or cut the front section off the grocery bag. Although it may have writing on one side, the front is easier to use because there are no seams.

2. Tear around the edges to give a jagged edge. Shape it like a skin if you wish.

3. Crumple the paper into a ball, press it together tightly, and open it up. Repeat several times. Smooth it out with your hand.

4. Rub the entire piece of paper with the side of a brown crayon. Use the leftover piece of grocery bag to protect the table from crayon marks, as you want to go over the edge of the "skin".

5. Draw pictures on the paper to represent years or days. The illustrations usually started at the center and continued in a spiral. It is helpful to draw the spiral lightly in pencil first.

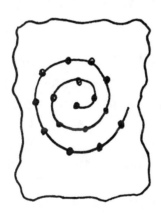 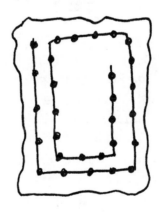

Variations

Make a class winter count. Use a grocery bag or a larger piece of brown kraft paper. Prepare the "hide" first with crayon. Work over several weeks or a month. Add a picture for each day. It can represent something that happened at school or in current events. Have the class decide on the pictures as a group or have individual or small groups of students be responsible for different days.

Create a winter count for the life of an imaginary Dakota boy or girl, a particular period in history, or the events in a book.

Use color. While the Dakota winter counts were primarily to record events, more decorative works on buffalo hides were made by many Native American residents of the plains. Some were used as robes or tepee covers. Many skins told the story of one particular event or used symbolic drawings to represent an individual or family.

Suggested Readings

The Legend of the Indian Paintbrush, Tomie dePaola. New York: Putnam, 1988. The legend of how the flower, the Indian Paintbrush, got its name tells the story of a young boy who finds his calling as an artist painting on buffalo hides.

Dancing Tepees: Poems of American Indian Youth, Virginia Driving Hawk Sneve, ed. New York: Holiday House, 1989. These poems by American Indian youth are based on the traditions of their cultures and include a Dakota Elk Song and an Osage Prayer Before Young Man's First Buffalo Hunt.

Time Line Accordion

Mexico and Central America

Historical chronicles and genealogies, as well as ritual calendars and tribute lists, were the main subjects of the accordion books of the Aztecs and the Mayans. The books were made from folded deerskin or bark paper. They were often coated with gesso to give a smooth white surface. Small pictures called glyphs were the writing. The drawing to the left is the glyph for the Aztec king Montezuma. There were also vibrant illustrations in rich colors.

This project is based on the Aztec and Mayan books in theme and basic form but adds a ribbon woven through the pages to act as a time line. This project is one that crosses many grade levels. It's the one I use when I work with groups of fifty first graders. It's easy for the students but does involve more preparation by the teacher. The slits are cut in the paper before the students begin. The books illustrated here were made by second graders, who were studying American biographies. The time lines can also describe historical periods and personal or family histories. Because the size of the book limits the amount of space for drawings and writing, the students need to be concise.

Materials:

Light oak tag or heavy paper, 5 1/2" x 17"

Ribbon 1/4" or 3/8" wide or yarn in 36" lengths

Pattern for cutting slits, glued to 5 1/2" x 17" oak tag

Tools:

Glue stick and scrap paper

X-acto knife or razor blade

Scrap cardboard for cutting surface

Markers or colored pencils

Materials per student:

1 piece 5 1/2" x 17" paper with slits

1 piece ribbon or yarn, 36" long

To Prepare Ahead

1. Gather the information for the time line. It can be a historical time period, a personal or family history, a biography, or the story line of a book. Eight dates will fit comfortably in the book. The amount of explanatory text should be limited as the pages are small.

2. Make the pattern for cutting the slits. Make two copies of the pattern on the following page. Cut out both of them. Glue the copies to one piece of 5 1/2" x 17" oak tag. Reverse the direction for the second copy. Cut slits in the pattern with an X-acto knife or razor blade. Make sure you have scrap cardboard underneath.

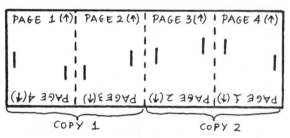

3. Place the pattern on top of one sheet of student book paper with a piece of cardboard underneath. Move the knife or razor through the slits in the pattern to make the slits in the student book paper. You might be able to cut through more than one sheet of student paper at a time. Experiment.

Pattern for Cutting Slits

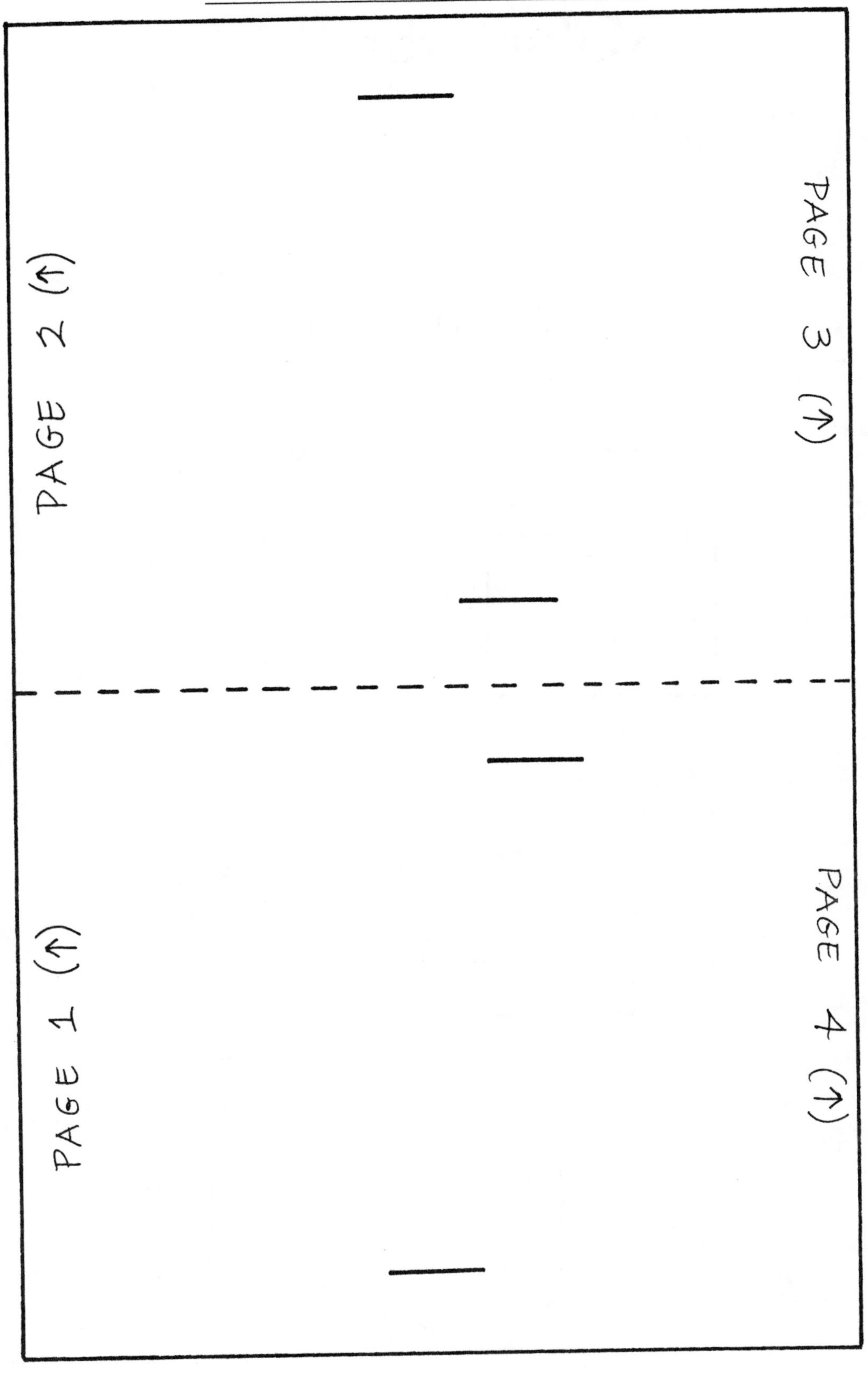

PAGE 3 (↑)

PAGE 2 (↑)

PAGE 1 (↑)

PAGE 4 (↑)

Making the Book

1. To fold paper into four pages that open like an accordion:
    a. Fold the paper in half.

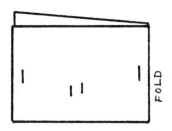

    b. Fold the top half in half by bringing the edge to meet the fold.

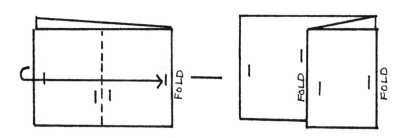

    c. Turn the paper over and do the same to the other half.

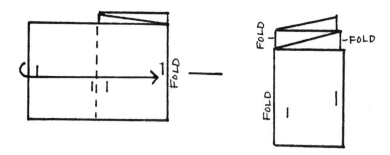

    d. The paper is now folded into four pages and the book will open like an accordion.

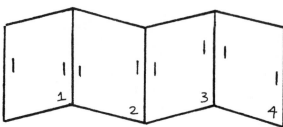

2. To thread the ribbon through the slits:

   a. Fold up the book so that the edge of the paper is on the right side and the fold is on the left. Start with the slit on the right. Push the ribbon through Slit A. Open the book and pull about 6" of the ribbon through.

   b. Push the ribbon through Slit B.

   c. Turn the book over and push the ribbon through Slit C.

   d. Turn the book over again, pull some ribbon through, and push the ribbon through Slit D.

   e. Repeat the process until the ribbon is threaded through all the slits. Be careful not to miss any slits.

3. Pull the ribbon through so that there is an even amount extending beyond the edges on both sides.

4. Open the book and make sure that the ribbon runs across the face of each page. If the ribbon has been started on the wrong side, only a little bit of ribbon will show. If that has happened, it's easy to correct by rearranging the folds so that the ribbon runs across the face of the page.

5. Write the text and draw the illustrations. The back of page 1 can be used for the title.

6. To close the book, wrap each end of ribbon around the book in the opposite direction. Tie in a single knot or a bow on the opposite side.

Variations

Make longer time lines. For books with more pages, follow the directions for making a Curandero Book on page 63.

Work together on a large time line. Use large paper that can be folded, or use a separate sheet for each page. Sheets of posterboard or cardboard can be attached together in the back with wide pieces of tape. There should be a slight gap between the sheets when they are taped so that the book will open and close easily.

Make gift books. Use the threaded ribbon as a design element in a book-card for Valentine's Day, Christmas, Mother's or Father's Day, etc. I first did this style of book as a valentine. When I discussed possible book projects with my son's preschool teacher, she looked at the valentine and said, "Hand-eye coordination." The class made dinosaur time lines and the project was underway.

Suggested Readings

The Flame of Peace: A Tale of the Aztecs, Deborah Nourse Lattimore. New York: HarperTrophy, 1987. A young Aztec boy, Two Flint, braves nine evil demons and brings the magic flame of peace to his people. The illustrations by the author are inspired by the Aztec manuscripts. The page numbers are written in Aztec as well as Arabic numerals.

Rain Player, David Wisniewski. New York: Clarion Books, 1991. A Mayan boy must defeat Chac, the god of rain, in a ball game to end the drought and escape the fate of being turned into a frog. The author has illustrated the book with dramatic cut-paper illustrations. The story begins with a picture of an old priest holding an accordion book.

Comic Book
U.S.A.

In the twentieth century, the United States has become known for the popular culture it exports throughout the world. American jazz, rock music, and films have all had a major influence. The comic book can be considered the book form of popular culture. While there are many precursors to the comic book, from the Aztec codices to the penny dreadfuls in 19th century England and color print books in Japan, the comic book as we know it began in the 1930's. Pulp magazines and comic strips in newspapers led the way. The comic book was created at Eastern Color Printing in New York, which printed the color funnies for Sunday newspapers. The color presses were underutilized much of the time. Harry Wildenberg folded a color printed newspaper sheet into a booklet and created the comic book. The first comic books were reprints of comic strips. Their success led to new characters and stories, created just for the comic books.

These books were made by third graders. From rough drafts through editing to the final copy, this project was a major undertaking for the students. While planning and executing this eight-page booklet is involved, the assembly of the book is simple. I have done it with many groups, from first grade up. I have the class work as a whole and go through the process step by step.

Materials:

11" x 17" white paper

Tools:

Scissors

Pencils, pens, and/or markers

Materials per student:

1 sheet of white paper, 11" x 17"

To Prepare Ahead

Plan and write drafts of the comic book. There are eight pages in the book. The layout can use all eight pages for the story or be six pages, with a front and back cover. Students can fold and cut extra blank books for their planning and drafts or work on separate sheets of paper. Comic books cover a wide range of stories from superheroes to Archie. Students can create their own characters, use myths from different cultures as a source, or write about local heroes who make the community a better place.

Making the Book

1. Discuss the two kinds of folds that will be used in making this book: hot dog folds and hamburger folds. It may sound silly, but it works. When you fold the paper in half in a hot dog fold, the paper forms a long rectangle. When you fold the paper in half in a hamburger fold, the paper forms a shorter rectangle that is closer to a square.

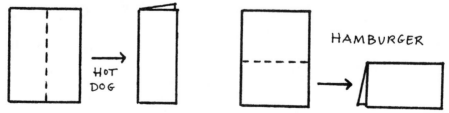

2. Fold the paper in half in a hot dog fold.

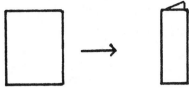

3. Open and fold in half in a hamburger fold.

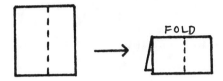

4. Leave the paper folded and fold in half again in a hot dog fold.

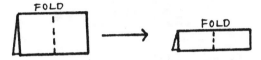

5. Hold the paper so that it forms a tent. The tent has two sides, one with a folded edge and one with open edges.

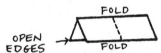

6. At the folded side, cut along the center fold to the peak of the tent. Make sure you go right to the top; that is, the fold.

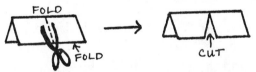

7. Open all the way up and refold to make the hot dog you started with. Smooth along the fold with your hand.

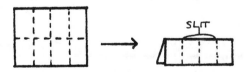

8. Hold the two ends and push in so that the center slit opens into a diamond. Keep pushing the two sides together until the diamond flattens out and the two side sections touch. Bring all the sections together and smooth along the fold.

9. Write the text and draw the illustrations.

Variations

Vary the size. Use standard 8 1/2" x 11" paper for a small book with 2 3/4" x 4 1/4" pages. Use 8 1/2" x 14" legal paper for a book with 3 1/2"x 4 1/4" pages. Use larger paper for larger books.

Use different colored papers. Try a dark background with light colored pencils for a dramatic effect. Choose colors appropriate to the story: orange marker on yellow paper for a fire-throwing superhero, blue marker on light green paper for creatures from under the sea.

Publish the comic books. Use standard size papers that fit in most copiers, 8 1/2" x 11", 8 1/2" x 14", and 11" x 17". Students make the books and do the writing and drawing with black pen or marker. The books are opened up to become a flat sheet of paper again. All the writing and drawing is on the same side. The paper is placed on the copier. The printed sheets of paper are folded and cut to make books for sharing.

Suggested Reading

Wingman, Daniel Pinkwater. New York: Dodd, Mead, 1975. Chinese American Donald Chen escapes from his troubles at school by reading comics under the George Washington Bridge. Wingman, a comic hero come to life, and a new teacher help Donald discover new abilities and make friends.

Curandero Book

Mexico

Curandero books are made by the healers of the Otomi Indians in the village of San Pablito, Mexico. The healers use bark paper cut-outs of figures that represent both benevolent and malign forces in the world, with the plant spirits of fertility often merging with Catholic symbolism. These accordion books describe the figures that are used in the healing. The bark paper, called amate, is made from the inner bark of the fig tree. It is the same paper that was made by the Aztecs and Mayans for their books. Strips of the inner bark are boiled in lye and water to soften, laid out in a grid on a flat stone, and pounded with a board until the fibers mesh together. The paper is used for the pages and the cover of the books, as well as for the figures.

This project uses the curandero book for inspiration but takes a less mystical approach. The students made books describing what heals their spirits and makes them feel better when they are sad. The cut-outs were made from brown bags and the books were eight pages long. When all sixteen projects were exhibited together, these books, made by fifth graders, elicited the strongest response from the viewers.

Materials:

Lightweight paper, 5 1/2" x 17", off-white or light tan preferred

Brown heavy paper (cover stock) or light cardboard, 4 1/2" x 6"

Brown bags or kraft paper, cut into 4" squares

Tools:

Scissors

Glue stick and scrap paper

Black pen or marker

Materials per student:

2 sheets of paper, 5 1/2" x 17"

2 sheets cover paper, 4 1/2" x 6"

4" squares of brown bags or craft paper

To Prepare Ahead

Write drafts of text. There will be eight pages with illustrations so the text does not have to be long. One sentence per page is sufficient. Students write about the things they do or think about to make them feel better when they are sad: talking to a friend, going for a walk, reading a book, riding a bike, remembering a particularly happy time. The illustrations may be planned now or later.

Making the Book

1. Fold tabs on each sheet of paper. The tabs should be about 3/4" wide. They should both be the same size.

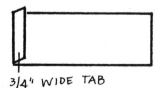

3/4" WIDE TAB

3/4" WIDE TAB

2. To fold each sheet of paper into fourths to make an accordion:

  a. Fold the paper in half with the tab on the inside.

  b. Fold the top half in half by bringing the edge back to meet the fold.

  c. Turn the paper over and do the same to the other half.

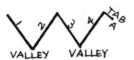

3. Open out the two sections so that each forms two valleys and a tab. The tabs will both be on the right side.

4. To attach the top of Tab A to the back of page 5:

  a. Fold up the first section with Tab A on top. Use two sheets of scrap paper. Insert one between page 4 and the rest of the pages. Place the second sheet on top of the pages and under Tab A.

b. Using glue stick, cover the entire tab with a thin coat of glue. Go over the edges onto the scrap paper.

5. Remove the scrap paper. Keep the first section folded with Tab A on top. Fold up the second section. Hold it in the same position as the first section with Tab B on top. Place the second section on the first, lining up the edges. Press to adhere.

6. Cut off Tab B. To make a longer book, do not cut off Tab B. Make a third section and glue it to Tab B. Continue for more sections. Cut off the last tab.

7. To check if the seam from attaching the tab is on the back of the book:
    a. Stand up the pages to form four valleys. The seam should ***not*** be visible from the top.

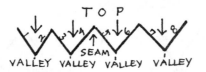

    b. If the seam is visible, the folds must be refolded in the opposite direction. Fold the first fold in the opposite direction. Continue with the rest. Make four valleys again to make sure that the seam is correct.

8. To attach the front cover to the back of page 1:
    a. Fold up the pages. Slide scrap paper between page 1 and the rest.

b. Using glue stick or paste and brush, cover the entire back of page 1 with a thin coat of glue. Go over the edges and onto the scrap paper. Remove and discard the scrap paper.

c. Place the folded pages, glue side down, on the back of the front cover. The cover is larger than the pages. There should be an even border all around. Press firmly. Open the pages and smooth down.

 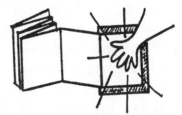

9. Repeat the process for the back cover. The back cover should be evenly lined up with the front cover.

10. Write the text on the pages and make the illustrations from the brown squares. The traditional papercuts from San Pablito are all symmetrical. If you wish to make symmetrical papercuts, fold the paper in half and cut designs. Try to cut the illustrations directly from the paper without drawing them first.

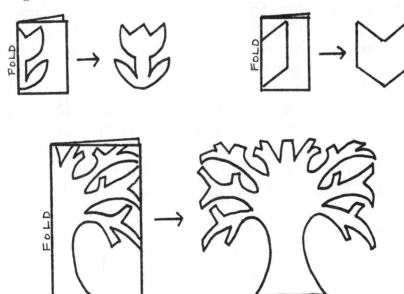

Variations

For younger students or quicker projects, make four-page books from one sheet of paper. Draw pictures with brown marker instead of cutting them from brown paper.

Add yarn or ribbon before attaching the back cover, following the directions in *Seasons Accordion Book* on page 88.

Think about what things in the world need healing—sick and hungry children, areas of the world in war and conflict, the environment—and make healing books for them. Students can make individual books or collaborate in small groups or as a class. More sections can be added if necessary. Because the folding and gluing of the sections are not always done precisely, the books tend to get wider as more sections are added. For a long book, cut the covers at the end to fit the pages.

Suggested Readings

The Cuckoo's Reward: A Folk Tale from Mexico in Spanish and English, Daisy Kouzel. Garden City, New York: Doubleday and Company, Inc., 1977. The cuckoo is a gray bird with a limited song who lays her eggs in the nest of other birds. This folk tale from Mexico tells how the cuckoo lost her beautiful plumage and sweet song in the struggle to save the seeds for new crops from destruction by the god of fire. The other birds care for her young in gratitude.

The Mouse Bride: A Mayan Folk Tale, Judith Dupre. New York: Alfred A. Knopf, 1993. This is a beautifully illustrated telling of a folktale that is told in various versions around the world. Two mice seek the most powerful being in the universe to marry their daughter. They are sent from the Sun, to the Cloud, to the Wind, to the Wall, who tells them that the mouse is the most powerful of all because he can make the Wall crumble from his burrowing.

Asia

Historical Overview,
page 71

Projects

India, Indonesia, Southeast Asia:
Palm Leaf Sequence Book,
page 75

The history of the book begins in western Asia. The earliest books were tablets of clay from Mesopotamia in about 4000 B.C. The writing was done on soft clay tablets with a reed stylus. The writing, cuneiform, was a series of wedge-shaped marks that evolved from pictograms. The soft clay was hardened in the sun to make durable books. There were legal documents, texts on astronomy, medicine, poetry, and religious matters. Their value to society is clear from the care they were given. They were stored in libraries and carefully indexed.

Two other traditions in western Asia use animal skin as their primary material: the scrolls of the Hebrews and the books of Persia and Arabia that use the Western codex style of binding. The Hebrew scrolls, made of leather and, later, vellum, were mounted on two rods. The form is still used today for writing the Torah. The books of Persia and Arabia were written first on vellum or parchment and later on paper. The Koran was written this way, but these books were also used for secular subjects.

Our projects will concentrate on the books of eastern Asia. Probably the richest book tradition, in terms of variety of form, is that of China. The development of books in China, from the scroll onward, spread to Japan and Korea.

The first books, *jian ce*, or slat books, were made of strips of wood or bamboo bound together by cord. They date from about 1700 B.C. and were in use until the fourth century A.D. The writing was done with a brush and ink. Some strips were long and narrow, 1/2" by 24". These would have been rolled up when not in use. Some were wider, from 1" to 2", and these would have been folded accordion style. The fact that Chinese is written vertically, from top to bottom, is attributed to the shape of these early books.

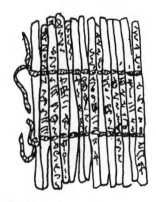

The slat book gave way to scrolls made of silk. Although silk was a more expensive material, it was more convenient to carry and to store. The end of the scroll was attached to a wooden roller with decorated tips. A blank piece of silk was attached to the beginning to act as a cover, protecting the rolled scroll. Silk was gradually replaced by the less expensive paper, the invention of which is attributed to Cai Lun in A.D 105.

In another shift toward convenience, the scroll evolved into the accordion book, when the paper was folded rather than rolled. The accordion books were easier to store and to use. Trying to find a particular passage

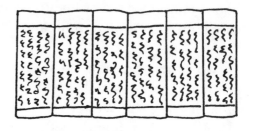

in the middle of a scroll involved a lot of rolling and unrolling. The accordion book came into prominent use in the mid-ninth century, primarily for writing the Buddhist scriptures, which are called *sutras*. Its Chinese name, *ching-che-chuang*, means sutra binding.

The next step in the evolution of books in China was to a book of folded and sewn leaves. Several transitional styles led the way to the

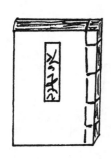

stitched binding of the Ming Dynasty in the sixteenth century. These books are made by folding sheets of paper in half, stacking the sheets individually, and sewing them together with the fold opposite the spine. The stitching is visible. The books were all soft cover, and each chapter of a book would be bound separately, with the entire set of volumes comprising the book. They were often stored between boards or in cases and laid flat on bookshelves. This style was in prominent use until the mid-twentieth century when it began to be replaced by Western bindings.

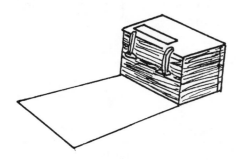

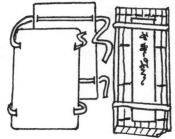

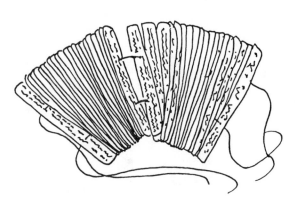

*T*he other main center of book development in eastern Asia was India. The primary form, made of palm leaves strung together, was in common use by the end of the fourth century. The leaves of the palm tree were cut in rectangular shapes, boiled in water or milk, dried, and rubbed with a shell or stone to make them smooth. The writing was most often done with a metal stylus. The writing was incised into the leaves. Ink was rubbed over the leaf, then wiped off. It remained in the incised writing. The reason for the rounded character of Indian scripts is because straight horizontal strokes would have split the leaves. The leaves have one, two, or three holes and are strung on cords. Coins, rings, or beads tied to the ends of the cords keep the book together. Some books have decorated wooden covers.

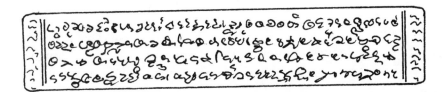

This palm leaf form spread to Indonesia and Southeast Asia. Even when different materials were used, such as bamboo in Indonesia and lacquered cloth, ivory, and metal in Southeast Asia, the long rectangular shape remained. Books of a similar shape were also made in Tibet. There, unattached paper pages were stacked between wooden covers that were then wrapped in cloth. The accordion form was also used in India and Southeast Asia.

Palm Leaf Sequence Book

India, Indonesia, Southeast Asia

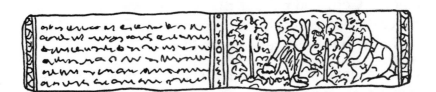

Rectangular books of palm leaves are the traditional form of India, Indonesia, and Southeast Asia. The leaves have one, two, or three holes and are strung together on a cord. Knots, rings, or beads at each end of the cord keep the book together. I have used this project often with first and second graders. The book contains four pages, a title page followed by three pages with a text that creates a sequence. I keep it simple with one hole so that there will only be two knots to tie, one at each end of the cord. I have used both ribbon and yarn for the cord. Ribbon is easier to thread through the beads. Curling ribbon for wrapping packages works well. The cord is long enough for the pages to spread out for display on a bulletin board or table. The narrow width of the strips is traditional and makes the use of a hand-held one-hole punch possible. The page layout is inspired by the page from an Oriya manuscript from India (see page 75). Borders divide the pages into halves, one for text and one for illustrations.

Materials:

Strips of heavyweight paper or oak tag, 1 3/4" x 8"

Thin ribbon, yarn, or string, 12" lengths

Pony Beads
(Plastic craft beads with large holes)

Tools:

Hole punch

Awl or nail and hammer (optional)

Black and color markers or pencils

Materials per student:

4 strips of heavy paper or oatag, 1 3/4" x 8"

1 piece ribbon or yarn, 12" long

2 pony beads

To Prepare Ahead

1. Using the pattern on the opposite page, make patterns for punching the holes. Copy and cut out the pattern. For longevity, glue it to a heavier piece of paper. Punch the hole with a hole punch. The more patterns you have, the faster the project will go.

2. Prepare drafts of text. There will be a title page and three pages with one sentence each, or two if the writing is small. The book will tell the story of a sequence. Possible starting points: yesterday, today, tomorrow; last week, this week, next week; breakfast, lunch, dinner; morning, afternoon, evening. The easiest way to make the transition from rough draft to finished book is for the students to write each sentence on a separate strip of paper. Illustrations can be planned now or when the book is being made.

Making the Book

1. Place the pattern on each of the four strips and trace around the hole with a pencil.

2. Punch the holes in the strips.

Pattern

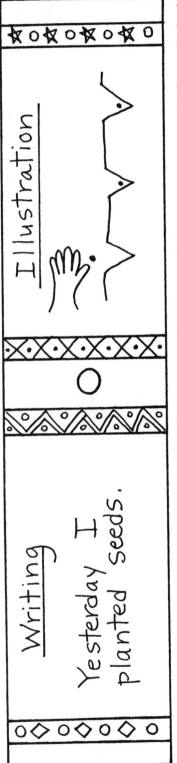

3. Draw the lines for the borders on each page using the pattern as a guide. There should be two lines on either side of the center hole and two at each edge. Designs can be added between the lines.

4. Write the sentences and draw illustrations on each page. The text should be on the left side, the images on the right. The pattern has an example.

5. Place the pages in order.

6. **a.** Put the ribbon through the hole in the bead.
b. Tie a knot at one end of the ribbon. **c.** Tighten the knot around the bead. **d.** Tie a second knot to secure it. Tug on the bead to tighten the knot.

7. Starting with the end of the ribbon without a bead, push the ribbon through the holes in the pages. The ribbon can be strung through the holes one page at a time or all at once if the holes are aligned.

8. On the other end of the ribbon, tie a double knot with the bead inside.

9. Read the book by flipping the pages forward. Because there is only one center hole, the pages can spin around. A page that is upside down is no cause for panic. Just spin it around to get it right side up.

10. To close the book: Wrap the ribbon or yarn around the book and tuck the bead under it.

Variations

Make books with longer strips of 1 3/4" x 12" and punch three holes, one in the center, one 1" from the left edge, and one 1" from the right edge, all centered top to bottom.

Make books with two holes. Using the 1 3/4" x 12" strips, punch one hole, 1 1/2" from the left edge, and one 1 1/2" from the right edge, both centered top to bottom.

Use for book reports. Use separate pages for beginning, middle, and end; who, what, where, when, why; significant events in the plot; character descriptions, etc.

For science, make palm leaf books to write up experiments. Make a book of the planets on black paper. Make a weather book or a cloud book, with blue paper and a separate page for each kind of cloud formation.

Make a rainbow book with every page a different color.

Make a fan book. Punch the holes at one end of the pages, rather than in the middle. Stack pages and thread yarn or ribbon through holes. Tie two ends of yarn in a double knot. Do not tie knot tight up against the pages or the pages won't fan. Add beads for decoration.

Work with larger pages so that more text can be written. If the page is wider than 1 3/4", a regular hole punch will not work. In this case, the holes are made last. The pages, with text and illustration, are stacked in order and clipped together. The holes are made in all the pages at once with a nail or awl and hammer. Don't forget to put a piece of wood underneath to protect the table.

Suggested Readings

The Elephants and the Mice: A Panchatantria Story, Marilyn Hirsh. New York and Cleveland: World Publications 1970. The Panchatantria (Five Books) is a collection of hundreds of stories gathered in India over two thousand years ago. This story tells of the friendship and cooperation of the mice and the elephants.

Usha, the Mouse-maiden, Mehlli Gobhai. New York: Hawthorn Books, Inc., 1969. This is another Panchatantria story.

Silent Lotus, Jeanne M. Lee. New York: Farrar, Straus and Giroux, 1991. This beautifully illustrated story, set in long-ago Cambodia, tells of a young girl who cannot hear or speak and becomes the most famous dancer in the Khmer court.

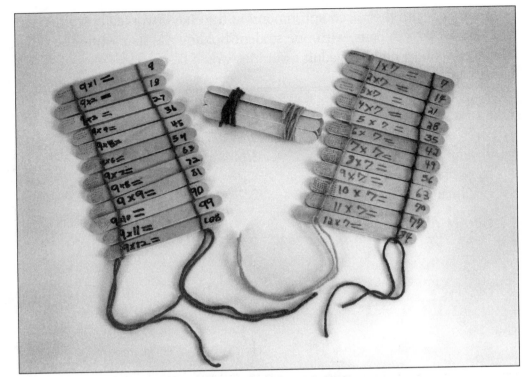

Math Slat Book

Ancient China

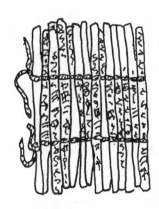

China's earliest book form, the slat book, serves as the basis for this project. One of the primary functions of early books in all cultures was mathematics. Books were used to keep records of property owned and traded, business transactions, and tributes offered to kings and emperors. One historical example is an inventory of weapons from A.D. 93 to 95 during the Han Dynasty. The entire inventory contains 77 wooden strips, each 9" high and 1/2" wide.

This project uses the slat book to make study guides for multiplication tables or other math exercises. While the idea of how to put this book together is simple, the assembly can be tricky because the knots must be tied tightly against the slats to keep the book together. I have made these books several times with third graders, including the ones in the photograph. They started slowly, and some struggled a bit with the knots, but all were pleased with their accomplishments at the end. It worked best when the students worked in pairs, with one student holding the slats while the other tied. For younger children, adult assistance would be needed.

Materials:

Tongue depressors or large craft sticks or cardboard strips, 3/4" x 6"

Yarn or ribbon in 40" lengths

Tools:

Marker or pencil

Elmer's type glue

Materials per student:

10 - 12 craft sticks or cardboard strips, 3/4" x 6"

2 pieces of yarn or ribbon, each 40" long

Making the Books

1. Fold each piece of yarn in half.

2. Insert a slat in the fold of one piece of yarn, so that the yarn is about 1 1/4" from the left-hand end of the slat. Tie a single knot, making sure that the knot is at the bottom of the slat. Pull on the yarn so that the knot is tight against the slat. The yarn should grip enough to stay in place while you tie a second knot, making a double knot.

3. Using the same procedure, tie the second piece of yarn around the slat, about 1 1/4" from the right-hand end of the slat.

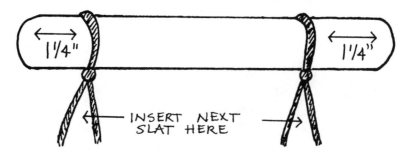

← INSERT NEXT
SLAT HERE

4. Insert the next slat between the pieces of yarn and tie double knots, following the procedure for tying knots. You may find it easier if the slat you are tying is close to the edge of the table or desk.

5. Repeat until all the slats are tied together.

6. Write in the numbers. This is particularly useful for multiplication tables but can be used for addition, subtraction, and division as well.

    The yarn divides the slat into sections. For example, 5 x 5 = can go in the center section; 25 can go in the right section. Five rows of 5 dots, to correspond to 5 x 5, can go in the left section. The rows of dots work well for the smaller numbers but are difficult to fit for the larger numbers.

7. Use glue to rescue books in which the knots are not tied tightly enough. A little dab of white glue, applied neatly with a toothpick, will help keep yarn in place.

8. To close the book: Either fold the slats like an accordion or roll the slats like a scroll. Any extra yarn can be wrapped around the book.

9. To use for studying: Students can use the books to test themselves by holding their thumbs over the answers.

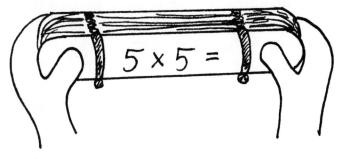

Variations

For visual interest, paint the slats with different color tempera or acrylic paint before tying them together. Or use different color poster board strips.

Make larger size math slat books, using pieces of poster board or cardboard, to hang on the wall. There now will be room for the rows of dots. Use drawn dots, stickers, cut-paper shapes, or rubber stamps. The end of a pencil eraser and stamp pad make great dots.

Collaborate on a class book. Each student writes his or her name on a slat and decorates it to reflect his or her personality and interests. Write names horizontally for a book that can hang on the wall; vertically, for a book that can stand like an accordion on a table.

Make name books with one letter per slat. Write a name acrostic with one line per slat—e.g., *Jen: J is for joy. E is for excellence. N is for noble.*

One successful project I did was a "Life in the Sea" book. Light blue poster board strips were tied with green yarn. Students drew pictures, wrote descriptions, and worked with rubber stamps and handmade stencils. To make the stencils, I traced pictures from books, transferred them to poster board, covered the board with clear contact paper for longevity, and cut out the stencils with an X-acto knife.

Suggested Readings

A Grain of Sand, Helena Clare Pittman. New York: Hastings House Publishers, 1986. An original story set in fifteenth-century China that reads like a folk tale. A humble peasant wins the hand of a princess in marriage by using math.

Count Your Way Through China, Jim Haskins. Minneapolis, Carolrhoda Books, Inc., 1987. Information about China presented through the numbers one to ten. One slightly jarring note is the illustration of "eight volumes" in which the books have Western bindings.

Seasons Accordion Book

China, also Japan and Korea

Accordion books with hard covers originated in China and spread to Japan and Korea. Traditionally, the books contained *sutras* (Buddhist scriptures) or were albums of calligraphy or painting. This project takes its inspiration from a contemporary accordion book purchased in Boston's Chinatown. Written in Chinese and English, it is called *Long Established Customs at Chinese Festivals*. Since many of the festivals are related to the seasons, they were chosen as the theme of the book.

The book is made first, and the text and illustrations are added at the end. I have made the blank book with fifty third graders in a little over twenty minutes, with two or three additional adults to help. I've also made the book with first and second graders without difficulty. The only real problem for older students seems to be limiting the text to fit the small size of the pages.

Materials:

Lightweight white paper, 5 1/2" x 17 for pages

Lightweight white paper, 3 1/4" x 4" for title strip

Heavy paper (cover stock) or light cardboard, 5 3/4" x 4 1/2" for covers

Yarn or ribbon, 24" lengths for tie

Tools:

Markers and/or pencils

Glue stick

Scrap paper

Masking tape (optional)

Materials per student:

1 piece 5 1/2" x 17" lightweight paper

2 pieces 5 3/4" x 4 1/2" heavy paper

1 piece 3 1/4" x 4" lightweight paper

1 piece of ribbon or yarn 24" long

To Prepare Ahead

Prepare drafts of the text. There will be four pages, one for each season. The text can center on natural occurrences, such as weather and growth cycles; on holidays celebrated; or on activities such as swimming, sledding, etc. The pages are small, so the text should be limited to three to five sentences, depending on their length and the size of the writing. A small illustration will go at the top of each page. The illustrations can be small detailed pictures or simple drawings that function as an emblem for the season. The name of the season can be written, or the pictures can serve as identification. A title piece will be pasted to the front cover. Students may also want to plan the title and cover illustration now.

Making the Book

1. To fold paper into four pages that open like an accordion:
   a. Fold the paper in half.

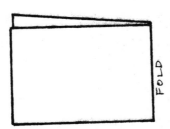

   b. Then, fold the top half in half by bringing the edge to meet the fold.

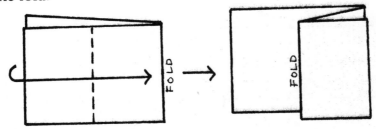

   c. Turn paper over and do the same to the other half.

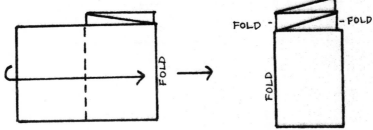

   d. The paper is now folded into four pages that open like an accordion.

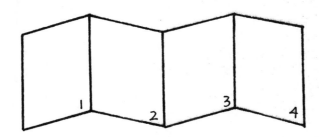

2. Optional: Make lines using the line guide.

   If you wish to use the line guide, make copies of the guide for the students. Students will place each page of the accordion over the guide and trace over the lines with pencil. If students have difficulty holding the papers and making the lines, the guide can be taped to the desk with masking tape. The book paper can then be taped to the guide with masking tape. Rulers can be used to get straighter lines. The rectangle at the top of the guide can be traced and used as a frame for the drawing, or the top section can be left blank and the drawing made without an outline. Be gentle when removing the masking tape.

3. If you have used the line guide, your folded paper will look like this.

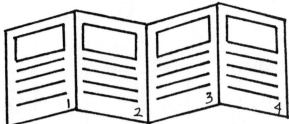

The writing and illustrations will be done after the covers are attached. The front cover will be glued to the back of page 1. The back cover will be glued to the back of page 4. A tie will be added before the back cover is glued.

4. To attach the front cover to the back of page 1:
   a. Fold up the pages. Open the first page. Insert scrap paper between page 1 and the rest of the pages. Close the first page so that the book is folded up again, this time with the scrap paper inside.

   b. Using glue stick, cover the entire back of page 1 with a thin coat of glue. Go over the edges and onto the scrap paper.

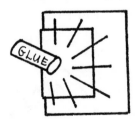

   c. Keeping the pages folded, remove and discard the scrap paper.

d. Place the folded pages, glue side down, on the back of the front cover. The cover is a little larger than the pages. There should be an even border all around. Press firmly. Open the pages and smooth down.

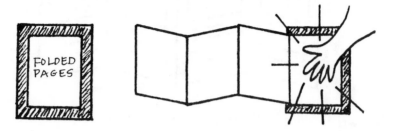

5. To add the tie and attach the back cover to the back of page 4:

a. Fold up the pages with the front cover face down. Open the back page. Insert a new sheet of scrap paper between page 4 and the rest of the pages. Close page 4 so that the book is folded up again, this time with the scrap paper inside.

b. Using glue stick, cover the entire back of page 4 with a thin coat of glue.

c. Keeping the pages folded, remove the scrap paper.

d. Place the ribbon or yarn across the center of the page, with the middle of the ribbon in the middle of the page. A good way to center the ribbon is to hold the book up and adjust the ends of the ribbon until they are even.

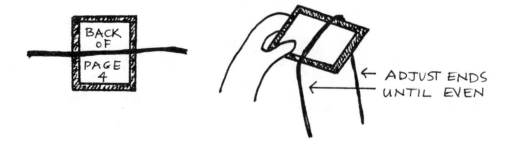

e. Place the inside of the back cover face down on the back of page 4. Make sure the front and back covers are lined up evenly. Press firmly. Open the pages and smooth down.

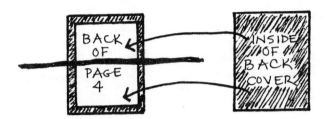

6. Write the text and draw the illustrations on the pages.

7. Write the title on the title strip and add illustrations if desired.

8. Glue the title strip to the front cover. Using glue stick and scrap paper, cover the entire back of the title strip with glue. Place it on the center of the front cover and smooth down.

9. To close book: Fold it up and tie it in front with a bow.

Variations

Different size paper may be used. The cover should be about 1/4" wider and 1/4" longer than the folded pages. This way, if the folding is not precise, there is still room for the pages to fit within the cover.

The books can contain additional pages. The Curandero book project on page 63 has directions for longer accordion books. A seasons book with eight pages would give room to alternate text and illustrations on separate pages.

A twelve-page book could be used for a Chinese New Year project, with one page for each sign of the zodiac. Since red is the traditional color of celebrations and the new year, red covers and red or gold cords would be especially appropriate.

Other subject ideas include the twelve months of the year, the twelve signs of the Western zodiac, a page or two-page spread for the planets, charting the growth of a plant, the life cycle of butterfly, etc. What I find especially appealing about accordion books is that when they are open, all the pages can be viewed at the same time. We get to see the whole story all at once, and they make for wonderful displays.

Suggested Readings

Dragon Kite of the Autumn Moon, Valerie Reddix. New York: Lothrop, Lee and Shephard, 1991. Kite day is celebrated on Taiwan on the ninth day of the ninth month. Kites, which are flown during the day, are set free at night to carry one's misfortunes away and burned on their return to earth. In this touching story, the young Tad-tin sacrifices his beloved dragon kite to help his ailing grandfather.

Yeh-Shen: A Cinderella Story from China, retold by Ai-Ling Louie. New York: Philomel Books, 1982. This Chinese Cinderella story, familiar from her childhood, was found by the author in an ancient Chinese manuscript.

The Rat, the Ox, and the Zodiac: A Chinese Legend, Dorothy Van Woerkom. New York: Crown Publishers, Inc., 1976. The emperor chooses the twelve animals of the zodiac, but Rat and Ox argue over who should be first. The case is decided by a test of strength versus wit.

Book of Haiku

Japan, also China, Korea, and Vietnam

In this project, pages of haiku or other short poetry are bound in the Oriental tradition. It is perhaps easiest to understand the Oriental binding by comparing it to the Western binding. Both start with pages that are folded in half. The Western binding sews a group of pages together along the fold. The Oriental binding sews a stack of individually folded pages together opposite the fold along the open ends, forming a pouch. Its Japanese name is *fukuro toji*, or pouch binding. This method of binding developed because very thin paper was used, and writing could be done on only one side.

Students may write their own haiku or other short poems or use the book as an exercise in literature appreciation and work with haiku by Japanese masters of the form. I did this project with sixth grade students. While some liked writing haiku more than others, they all enjoyed doing the collages to accompany their poems and found the process of binding very satisfying. I didthe binding with small groups of three to five students. The directions may look overwhelmingly long, but that's only because I've tried to break down the procedure into the smallest steps.

Materials:

8 1/2" x 11" lightweight white paper, such as 20 lb. copy paper, for pages

8 1/2" x 11" colored paper, such as 60 lb. colored copy paper, for covers

Strips of white paper for titles, 2 1/2" x 4"

Origami or other colored paper for illustrations

Embroidery floss, crochet cotton, or heavy thread, 34" lengths

Tools:

Scissors, Glue stick and scrap paper

Thin black marker or pen for writing text

Tapestry needle

Clothespins or paper clips

Nail or awl and hammer or block of wood

Piece of wood to protect table surface from awl or nail

Materials per student:

5 to 7 sheets of 8 1/2" x 11" white paper

2 sheets of 8 1/2" x 11" colored paper

1 strip of paper, 2 1/2" x 4"

1 piece of thread, 34" long, and needle

2 clothespins or paper clips

To Prepare Ahead

Write or collect 5 to 7 haiku or short poems. The information in this section on writing haiku comes from two sources: *The Haiku Handbook: How to Write, Share, and Teach Haiku* by William J. Higginson (McGraw Hill, 1985), which I recommend highly, and a conversation with poet Paul Marion of Lowell, Massachusetts, whose poems are quoted here. While many of us learned haiku as "three-line-seventeen syllable" poems, it is not necessary to observe these restrictions. The idea of haiku is to say a lot with a little. It is about writing images, or word pictures, and writing them briefly. Connecting and descriptive words are left out. There are no similes, metaphors, or other literary devices. The haiku shown here are all three lines. The three line form is used frequently and is a good starting point, but the poems can be shorter or longer.

While I don't consider myself particularly proficient at haiku, it seems easiest to describe the process through first-hand experience. I am in the garden, weeding. The sun is hot and I am not particularly happy. A butterfly lands on a leaf next to me. I think it is beautiful, and it reminds me why I have a garden and that I do like taking care of it. I write the following haiku:

> *Pulling weeds,*
> *hot sun. Next to me,*
> *a butterfly lands on a leaf.*

I don't describe my emotions or my thoughts. I write about what I see, hear, smell, feel, taste, or do. By creating a precise picture of what I respond to, I give the reader the potential to have that same experience. I step back and let the image do the talking.

Haiku often juxtaposes two contradictory thoughts. Sometimes they are two opposing thoughts or feelings within one event, as in the poem above. Others can be two separate events, as in the following haiku by Paul Marion. On the same day of the summer in 1991, there was a hurricane and the attempted overthrow of the president of the Soviet Union. These two events led to a series of haiku entitled "Haiku for Hurricane Coup."

> *The white dish spins-*
> *I keep looking*
> *for the neighbor's cat.*

In another haiku by Paul Marion, he creates a picture that we can see, hear, and feel.

> *Rain sings down*
> *the drain.*
> *Wet night/still.*

Another restriction that is often placed on haiku is that they must be about the seasons or nature. In classical Japanese haiku, the seasons were indicated by specific "season words." Contemporary haiku in both Japan and the West no longer require these indications. Students should look for moments in their own lives: in school; sports and games; interactions with their friends, family, and pets; even watching television. The poems in the book can all reflect on a similar theme, or they can have a variety of subjects.

Making the Book

1. One at a time, fold each sheet of white paper in half. Each sheet of folded paper has two sides and the potential for two pages, but only one side will be used here.

2. Before writing the haiku on the pages, make sure the paper is facing the proper direction. The fold should be on the right side. This is very important.

FOLD

3. Write the haiku on the pages, leaving space for illustrations. The illustrations can be above or below the writing or between the lines. The left-hand edge of the pages, the open side, will be sewn into the binding. It is important that there be no writing or illustration in this space. As a reminder, draw a pencil line 3/4" from the left-hand edge, or use the line guide on page 96. Copy and cut out the line guide. Place it inside the folded paper. Remember to keep the fold on the right-hand side.

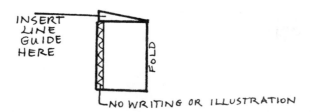

INSERT LINE GUIDE HERE

FOLD

NO WRITING OR ILLUSTRATION

4. Illustrate the haiku with a cut-paper collage.

   a. The illustrations can be abstract or representational. They can be as brief and concise as the haiku. Simple shapes—squares, circles, rectangles, triangles, and diamonds—can be used singly or in combination. The colors can help convey the meaning of the poem. Blues and greens are usually thought of as cool, calming colors and suggest sky, water, and growing things. Yellow, red, and orange are hot colors that suggest strong emotions, heat, and fire. If you wish to make representational pictures but are not comfortable with drawing, build them out of simple shapes. For example, four circles and a long oval can make a butterfly. Whether your shapes are simple or more complex, try to cut them directly without drawing them first. In workshops, I have found that many adults and children are reluctant to leave their pencils behind, but the results have always been excellent. There is a freshness and simplicity that comes from what Matisse called "drawing with scissors."

   b. Glue the illustrations to the pages with glue stick and scrap paper. Cover the back of each piece with a thin layer of glue. Go over the edges and onto the scrap paper. Discard the scrap paper after each use.

5. Write the title and add illustrations, as desired, on the strip of paper.

6. Fold the two sheets of cover paper in half, one for the front cover, one for the back. Fold them neatly, one at a time.

↑TOP↑

↑ OPEN EDGES ↑

DO NOT WRITE OR PLACE ILLUSTRATIONS IN THIS SPACE

FOLD →
↓

↓ BOTTOM ↓

7. On the front cover, draw a pencil line parallel to the left edge about 1/2" from the edge. The holes for the binding will be made along this line.

8. Glue the title strip to the front cover, using glue stick and scrap paper. The fold is on the right-hand side. Some of the left-hand edge will be sewn into the binding.

9. Neatly stack the pages in order. If you have used a wet glue for the collage, make sure it is dry first. Place the back cover on the bottom of the pile and the front cover on the top. Check to see that all the folds are on the same side. Hold the entire pile in both hands and tap against the table to make sure the stack is even. Clip it together with two clothespins or paper clips, one on the top edge and one on the bottom edge, about 2" from the unfolded edge of the book. The clips will stay on the book until the sewing is finished.

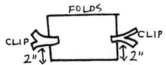

10. Place the clipped stack on a piece of wood to protect the table from the nail or awl. Make four holes through the stack along the pencil line by hitting an awl or nail with a hammer or a block of wood. The holes should be evenly spaced. They can be measured and marked first with a pencil or just done by eye.

11. Thread the needle. Do not tie a knot. The thread will be used singly, as in embroidery.

12. Start at the back of the book. Go through the top hole, Hole 1. Pull the thread through the hole until about 6" of thread is left. Place the thread under the clip to hold it in place while you sew.

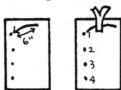

13. The basic principle of binding is to wrap the thread around the edges of the book at each hole. You will be going through the same hole more than once. Wrap the thread around the top of the book and go into Hole 1 again, entering from the back of the book. Pull the thread so that it is taut, but not digging into the edge.

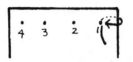

14. Wrap the thread around the side of the book and go through Hole 1 again, entering from the back of the book.

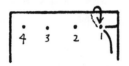

15. You have now wrapped all the edges you can at Hole 1. You are on the front of the book now. Go down to Hole 2.

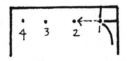

16. Go through Hole 2, entering from the front of the book. Wrap the thread around the side of the book and go through Hole 2 from the front again.

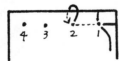

17. There are no more edges to wrap at Hole 2, so go to Hole 3. Go through Hole 3 from the back of the book. Wrap the thread around the side of the book and go through Hole 3 from the back again. You'll notice that there are some unfilled spaces. Don't worry. These will be filled later.

18. There are no more edges to wrap at Hole 3, so go to Hole 4. Go through Hole 4 from the front of the book. Wrap the thread around the side of the book and go through Hole 4 from the front again. Wrap the thread around the bottom edge of the book, and go through Hole 4 from the front again. You have now wrapped all the edges and sides of the book.

19. To get back to where you started to tie the two ends of thread together, go from Hole 4 to Hole 3, entering Hole 3 from the back of the book. Then go from Hole 3 to Hole 2.

20. Stop! It is time to tie the two ends of the thread together. Unclip the book and take the needle off the thread. Tie the two ends in a square knot with the knot over Hole 1. A square knot is a double knot. The first knot is done with the thread in your right hand on top, the second is done with the thread in your left hand on top. A diagram can be found on page 17 in the section on basic techniques. It can be a little tricky to keep the thread taut while tying the knot. Partners to hold the thread are helpful.

21. Cut extra thread, but make sure to leave at least 1/2". If the thread is cut too close to the knot, it can unravel.

Variations

For Younger children, use unfolded sheets of paper and a three-hole punch. Use yarn without a needle for sewing. If you wrap a little tape around the end of the yarn, it won't fray. Clip the book together and push the yarn through the holes. Because the yarn tends to slip off the top and bottom, wrap only the side edges.

This Binding lends itself to working with a computer. Use unfolded sheets of paper. Set margins on the computer so that there is room on the left for the binding.

Vary the materials. Use wrapping paper or handmade patterned paper for the covers. Make patterns with potato prints or rubbings of textured surfaces with the side of a crayon. Use a different colored paper for each page. Combine two colors of embroidery floss for interesting thread.

Make a book of leaf rubbings. Collect leaves from a local park or the school grounds. Fold the paper in half. Insert a leaf into the folded page. Rub both sides of the paper with the side of a crayon to make prints of both sides of the leaf. Remember that the fold will be on the right and that space needs to be left for the binding on the left side.

Make a Class Year Book. Each student writes and illustrates one 8 1/2" x 11" page about himself, leaving room on the left for the binding. The pages are copied on a copier. Each student gets one page from everyone in the class. She puts them together, makes covers, and binds the book.

Suggested Readings

In a Spring Garden, Richard Lewis, ed. New York: The Dial Press, 1965. Japanese haiku beautifully illustrated by Ezra Jack Keats with watercolor and collage.

Haiku-vision in Poetry and Photography, Ann Atwood. New York: Charles Scribner's Sons, 1977. This collection of haiku and accompanying photographs also includes a discussion of the spirit of haiku and photography.

In the Eyes of the Cat, selected by Demi. New York: Henry Holt and Company, 1992. This book contains a good selection of haiku and other short poetry from Japan about the seasons.

Europe

Historical Overview,
page 103

Projects

Scandinavia:
Viking Rune Stone,
page 105

Rome:
Pugillares,
page 109

15th & 16th Century Europe:
Newsbook,
page 113

Medieval Europe:
Medieval Book,
page 119

The history of the book in Europe begins in Africa, with the papyrus scrolls of Egypt. The use of papyrus as a writing material spread to Greece and Rome, where scrolls were the primary book form of the classical era. Our word *page* comes from the Latin word *pagineum*, which means "column on a scroll." The scrolls of Greece and Rome were all writing with no illustrations. One of the largest collections of scrolls was at the Alexandrian Museum and Library in Alexandria, Egypt. The founding of the library is attributed to Ptolemy II (283-247 B.C.). The library housed over 700,000 volumes of works of literature, philosophy, and science. Because the scrolls were written by hand, Alexandria became an important city for book production. We speak of getting a copy of a book. In the days of the handmade book, the way one got a copy was, in fact, to physically copy it, word for word, or hire a scribe to do the copying.

Parchment (treated animal skins) came to replace papyrus as a writing surface for books. The story is an interesting one. Around 200 B.C., the Egyptians stopped exporting papyrus. It is said that the Egyptian king was jealous of a new library in Pergamum, Turkey and afraid it might surpass the Alexandrian Library. The librarians at Pergamum looked for a substitute for papyrus and developed parchment. Writing had already been done on leather, but the surface was somewhat rough. The preparation of animal skins into parchment is a more involved process and results in a smooth writing surface.

With the invention of parchment came the evolution of the book from the scroll to the codex, or folded and sewn sheets. This basic form is the same style of book we use today, with sets of folded sheets gathered and sewn together along the fold. The earliest folded book extant is from the second century and is made of papyrus. Folded papyrus books did not hold up well and tended to crack along the folds. Parchment proved to be a more suitable material. Through the sixth century A.D., the papyrus scroll, the papyrus codex, and the parchment codex were all used, with the codex form favored by the Christians. After that time, the parchment codex became the preferred form. The folded parchment sheets were attached to wooden covers. These were then covered with leather or metalwork.

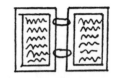

Because parchment and papyrus were both expensive, they were only used for works of lasting value. Accounts, correspondence, and rough drafts were done on wooden tablets that were covered with wax. The writing was scratched into the surface and could be erased when finished. These were used in Greece and Rome and continued to be used in Europe through the Middle Ages. The Greeks also wrote their notes on *ostraca*, which were pieces of broken pottery.

As Christianity spread throughout Europe, the parchment codex traveled with it. Every monastery had a *scriptorium* where monks copied the Bible and teachings of the early church. Latin was the common language. The writing was often embellished with decorated initial letters and borders. Books were also made for the courts of kings and princes. While the monks were writing on parchment in scriptoria, the Vikings were making their way through Europe and leaving their mark on stones with a form of writing called runes. In the twelfth century, book production became more widespread. Scribes and illuminators formed craft guilds and worked on commission for the new merchant class as well as the nobility.

As the demand for books continued to increase, production by hand could not provide a sufficient supply. The earliest printed books in Europe were done with woodcuts, which were originally developed by the Chinese. Text and illustrations were carved into wooden blocks in reverse, one block per page, inked, and then printed. Johannes Gutenberg invented movable metal type in Europe and produced the first printed Bible in 1455. The first copies were done on parchment, with colored initials and borders added by hand. His idea was to make a book that looked like a handmade one. As printing replaced handwritten books, new styles of lettering and page design developed. The history of books in Europe continued with innovations in type and paper and the mechanical processes of printing and binding. The basic form of the book, folded and sewn sheets, has remained constant.

Viking Rune Stone
Scandinavia

Rune stones were erected by the Vikings as memorial stones for the dead or, less frequently, as announcements of the accomplishments of the living. Most of the stones have been found in Scandinavia, but the seafaring ability of the Vikings led them to Germany, Britain, Russia and the Baltic countries, as well as Iceland, Greenland, Newfoundland, and the Near East. The memorial stones served two purposes, to pay tribute to the dead and as public notice that the death had occurred, rather like an obituary in the newspaper. The stones usually told who made the stone for whom and what the person's accomplishments had been. The writing, called runes, was carved into the stone. The runes were made up of vertical and diagonal lines. Because they were always carved in stone or wood, curved lines were hard to make, and horizontal lines wouldn't show up against the grain of the wood.

These stones were made by third graders. This was one of the, if not **the** most enjoyable project for the students. The writing was simple and the translation into runes was fun. They wrote on both sides of the paper stone, one side in English, the other in runes. After they had become familiar with writing runes on the paper stones, they wrote their names on rocks.

Materials:

Light brown or gray construction paper, oak tag, or posterboard, 9" x 12"

Rocks, as smooth as possible

Tools:

Scissors

Black marker

Black permanent marker for writing on rocks

Materials per student:

1 sheet 9" x 12" paper or oak tag

1 rock

To Prepare Ahead

Write the text in English. The usual wording was something like this: "Viking Prince made this stone for (or in memory of) his father, Viking King. He won many battles." Students can make the stones for family or friends, including pets; or famous people, living or dead; or fictional characters. Using the chart on the opposite page, transcribe the text into runes.

Making the Book

1. Cut the paper into a stone shape. The paper can be held horizontally or vertically. The bottom of the stone is usually flat.

2. Write the text on one side in English, and on the other side in runes. The writing was usually done between single or double lines. It is easiest to make the lines first, then do the writing in between. There were no spaces between words. A dot or a line indicated the end of one word and the beginning of the next. Designs were sometimes added, such as interlaced chains.

3. Write the name on the rock with permanent marker.

Rune Alphabet

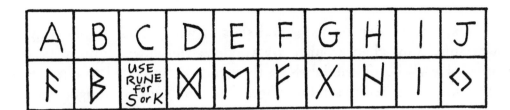

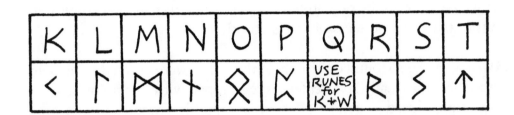

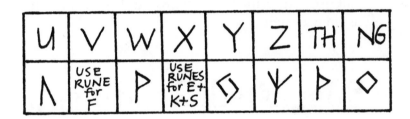

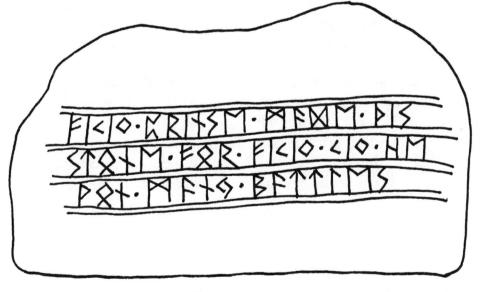

This stone says:
"Viking Prince made this stone for Viking King.
He won many battles."

Variations

Runes were written on twigs and slats of wood. Some runes showed ownership. A merchant would carry wooden strips in which his name was carved. He would tie the labels to the goods he intended to buy. Some rune sticks were used to send messages. Use craft sticks or tongue depressors. Write runes on the stick with a ball point pen. One that has run out of ink is preferable. Press hard to go into the surface of the stick. Rub over the stick with the side of a brown crayon. Students can write their names on the sticks or send messages to each other.

Runes were also found on thin gold discs that were derived from Roman coins. The discs, called *bracteates*, were stamped with designs and, in some cases, runes. Used as pendants or ornaments, they were sometimes worn for good luck. Cut circles from cardboard and cover them with yellow or gold paper. Students can write their names and good luck messages in runes, as well as draw designs.

Suggested Readings

Elfwyn's Saga, David Wisniewski. New York: Lothrop, Lee and Shephard Books, 1990. Elfwyn, born blind because of a curse carved in runes, saves her people from the greedy Gorm and receives her sight.

East of the Sun and West of the Moon, Mercer Mayer. New York: Macmillan Publishing Company, 1980. In this retelling of a Norwegian folktale, a maiden rejects a frog who turns out to be a prince and then rescues him from a troll princess with the help of the Moon, Father Forest, Great Fish of the Sea, and the North Wind. Beautiful illustrations, including the home of the North Wind, covered with rune carvings.

Pugillares
Rome

Pugillares were notebooks used in ancient Rome. The name comes from the Latin word *pugillus* meaning "fist," because the books were small enough to be held in the fist. Wooden tablets were covered with a coating of blackened wax. The writing was done in the wax with a metal stylus. The notebooks were used for writing rough drafts and correspondence and for figuring accounts. When finished, the wax was smoothed and ready for fresh writing. The tablets were tied together with leather cords. The use of these wax and wood tablets continued through the Middle Ages in Europe.

For this project, wax paper replaces the wax. Because some markers work better than others on the wax paper, you may want to experiment on scrap pieces first. These third grade students used the books to review Roman numerals.

Materials:

Heavy brown paper or light cardboard, 4 1/2" x 6"

Wax paper, about 6" x 12", torn from a 12" roll

Brown yarn in 6" lengths

Tools:

Pattern for cutting wax paper, 3 1/2" x 5"

Scissors

Glue stick and scrap paper

Hole punch

Black marker or pen

Materials per student:

2 pieces brown paper or cardboard, 4 1/2" x 6"

1 piece wax paper, 6" x 12"

2 pieces of brown yarn in 6" lengths

To Prepare Ahead

1. Make patterns for wax paper. Cut light cardboard into 3 1/2" x 5" pieces. Write on the pattern: Trace and cut two sheets of waxed paper per book. The project will go more quickly if there are several patterns.

2. Learn or review Roman numerals. 1-I, 2-II, 3-III, 4-IV, 5-V, 6-VI, 7-VII, 8-VIII, 9-IX, 10-X, 11-XI, 12-XII, 13-XIII, 14-XIV, 15- XV, 16-XVI, 17-XVII, 18-XVIII, 19-XIX, 20-XX, 30-XXX, 40-XL, 50-L, 60-LX, 70-LXX, 80-LXXX, 90-XC, 100-C, 200-CC, 300-CCC, 400-CD, 500-D, 600-DC, 700-DCC, 800-DCCC, 900-CM, 1,000-M

Making the Book

1. Punch two holes in each piece of brown paper. The holes can be measured or done by eye, but they need to be in the same place on both pieces. The holes should be about 1/4" from the top and bottom and 1/4" in from the edge. If the paper is thin enough, the holes can be punched through both sheets at once.

2. To cut two sheets of wax paper: Fold the wax paper in half. Place the pattern on the folded wax paper and trace the outline with marker. Cut out. Save the pattern, as you will use it again at the end.

3. To glue the wax paper to the brown paper:
   a. Arrange the brown paper so that the sides with the holes are next to each other.

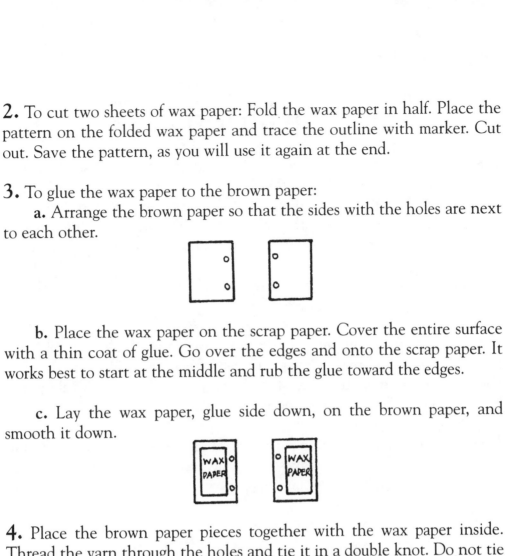

   b. Place the wax paper on the scrap paper. Cover the entire surface with a thin coat of glue. Go over the edges and onto the scrap paper. It works best to start at the middle and rub the glue toward the edges.

   c. Lay the wax paper, glue side down, on the brown paper, and smooth it down.

4. Place the brown paper pieces together with the wax paper inside. Thread the yarn through the holes and tie it in a double knot. Do not tie the knot tight up against the edge or the book will not open easily. Repeat for the second hole. Trim off the excess yarn after tying the knot.

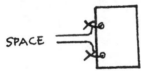

5. Write Roman numerals on wax paper inside the book. The book can be a reference guide to Roman numerals and list the numbers and their equivalents in Arabic numerals, or it can have math problems in Roman numerals. If you are using a marker, it is helpful to experiment first on scrap pieces of wax paper because some markers work better on wax paper than others.

6. Decorate the covers. To make them look like wooden tablets, trace around the pattern for cutting wax paper to make a border on the front and back covers. A title can be written on the front cover along with illustrations.

Variations

Use the books for correspondence. The wax paper doesn't work as well as wax and a stylus, but it can take a few erasures if the writing is done lightly with water-based marker. Students write messages on the wax paper and send the book to others. The other students read the messages, wipe off the marker with a damp paper towel, and write return messages.

Instead of yarn, use twist ties from bread. Follow the recycling theme and use cardboard cut from cereal boxes.

Pugillares often contained more than two pages. Make a book with multiple pages. Use regular paper instead of wax paper. Notice that the construction is similar to today's looseleaf binders. Write stories about the Roman gods and goddesses or reports about ancient Rome.

Use this method of attaching pages, with holes and ties, for an accordion book. For young children, make collage accordion books with twist ties. For books with durable pages, laminate the individual pages or cover them with clear contact paper.

Suggested Readings

Daughter of the Earth: A Roman Myth, Gerald McDermott. New York: Delacorte Press, 1984. This dramatic retelling of the Roman myth, based on the version in Ovid's *Metamorphoses*, tells the story of Ceres and her daughter, Proserpina, whose capture by Pluto, god of the Underworld, brings winter to the earth.

Pygmalion, Pamela Espeland. Minneapolis: Carolrhoda Books, Inc. 1981. In another myth from Ovid's *Metamorphoses*, Pygmalion, a sculptor who loves his art too much to have time for women and marriage, falls in love with a statue he makes. He is given happiness with his statue by Venus, the goddess of Love.

Two Roman Mice by Horace, Marilynne K. Roach. New York: Thomas Y. Crowell Company, 1975. A translation and retelling of Satire II by the Roman poet Quintus Horatius Flaccus (65-8 B.C.), this is the story of the country mouse and the city mouse. It combines cute drawings of mice with historical details.

Newsbook

Fifteenth & Sixteenth Century Europe

Newsbooks, also called relations, were the forerunners of newspapers. They came into being shortly after the invention of printing and covered a wide range of topics from explorations and discoveries to wars and natural disasters. The books were illustrated with woodcuts and some large initial letters in color. In 1493, Queen Isabella and King Ferdinand of Spain published Columbus's letter describing his discovery of America in a small booklet. It was translated from Spanish into Latin and German and published in separate editions in Rome, Paris, Florence, Antwerp, and Basel.

This project uses a simple unsewn booklet glued to a folded cover to make a newsbook. The books illustrated here were made by third graders. They enjoyed making the books but had some difficulty focusing on one particular historical event.

Materials:

Lightweight white paper, 11" x 17"

Heavy colored paper, 6" x 9", construction paper or cover stock

Tools:

Scissors

Glue stick and scrap paper

Pen, pencil, or marker

Materials per student:

1 sheet 11" x 17" white paper

1 piece 6" x 9" heavy paper

To Prepare Ahead

Plan and write drafts. The book will be about a particular event in history. The history can be personal, local, national, or international. A few possible subjects: explorations from Marco Polo to space, elections, wars, peace treaties, Nobel prizes, and sports events such as the Olympics and the World Series. There will be four to five pages of writing. It is helpful to do a final draft on paper the same size as the pages. Students can make extra sets of folded pages for their drafts.

Making the Book

1. Discuss the two kinds of folds that will be used in making this book: hot dog folds and hamburger folds. It may sound silly, but it works. When you fold the paper in half in a hot dog fold, the paper forms a long rectangle. When you fold the paper in half in a hamburger fold, the paper forms a shorter rectangle that is closer to a square.

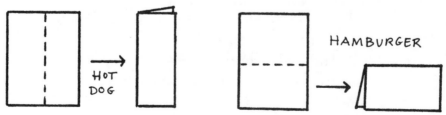

2. Fold the paper in half in a hot dog fold.

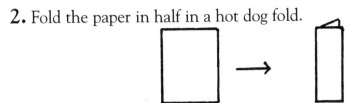

3. Open and fold in half in a hamburger fold.

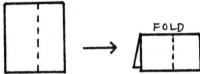

4. Leave the paper folded and fold in half again in a hot dog fold.

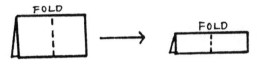

5. Hold the paper so that it forms a tent. The tent has two sides, one with a folded edge and one with open edges.

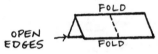

6. At the folded side, cut along the center fold to the peak of the tent. Make sure you go right to the top; that is, the fold.

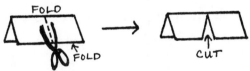

7. Open all the way up and refold to make the hot dog you started with. Smooth along the fold with your hand.

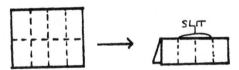

8. Hold the two ends and push in so that the center slit opens into a diamond. Keep pushing the two sides together until the diamond flattens out and the two side sections touch. Bring all the sections together and smooth along the fold.

9. Fold the heavy paper in half (hamburger fold) to form the cover.

10. To attach the front page to the front cover:
a. Insert scrap paper between the first page and the others.

b. Cover the entire surface with a thin coat of glue. Go over the edges and onto the scrap paper.

c. Remove and discard the scrap paper.

d. Place the pages inside the cover with the fold of the pages on the fold in the cover. The cover is bigger than the pages. There should be an even border of cover around the pages.

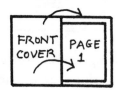

e. Close the book and press on the cover to adhere. Open the book and press on the page to adhere.

11. To attach the back page to the back cover:
a. Place the book with the front cover down. Insert the scrap paper between the last page and the rest of the book. Cover the entire surface with glue. Remove and discard the scrap paper.

 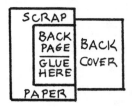

b. Close the book and press on the cover to adhere. Open and press on the pages to adhere.

12. Write the text in the book. Use the line guide if you wish. Copy and cut out the line guide. Insert it between the pages. Students may use the lines as they show through the paper or trace over them in pencil. Write on every line for small writing. Skip lines for larger writing. When skipping lines, put an *x* on the left side of the line to indicate which lines will have writing.

13. Write the title and the author on the cover. Illustrations are optional.

Variations

Add ribbon or yarn to make a tie. Before attaching the pages to the cover, lay a 24" length of ribbon or yarn across the middle of the cover. The center of the ribbon should be on the fold. Apply glue to the pages and attach the pages to the cover. The book can then be tied shut.

Make smaller books. With 8 1/2" x 11" paper, the cover paper will be 4 3/4" x 6 3/4". With 8 1/2" x 14" paper, the cover paper will be 4 3/4" x 7 3/4".

Publish the newsbooks. Use standard size copier paper, 8 1/2" x 11", 8 1/2" x 14", or 11" x 17". Fold and cut the pages. Do not glue them into the cover. Write the text in black marker or pen. Remember to leave the first and last pages blank as they will be glued to the cover. Open the pages to a single sheet and photocopy. Fold the copies into book pages and glue to the cover.

Make longer books. For a book with ten pages, use two sheets of paper. Fold each one into book pages. Glue the last page of one section to the first page of the second section. Glue the first and last pages to the cover. There will be a clump of pages glued to each other in the center. While this may not be an ideal form, it is a quick way to get a ten-page book without sewing.

Use the books for journals or short stories or for recording science experiments.

Suggested Reading

Fine Print: A Story about Johann Gutenberg, Joann Johansen Burch. Minneapolis: Carolrhoda Books, Inc., 1991. This story of how Gutenberg invented movable type gives an excellent view of city life in fifteenth-century Germany, as well as information on handwritten books, the making of paper, and the printing process.

Medieval Book
Medieval Europe

*I*n medieval times, books were made in monasteries and for royalty and nobility. They were handwritten with quill and ink on vellum (calfskin) and parchment (sheepskin) by scribes and bound between wooden covers. The covers were often covered with leather and sometimes metalwork and jewels. In the monasteries, the monks copied the Bible and other religious works. They decorated the pages with illuminated initials and borders. The nobility often commissioned elaborate books. One of the most common was the Book of Hours, with prayers and devotions to read throughout the days. These books also contained illustrations and information about each month of the year.

This is the most involved of all the projects. These sixth grade students chose from two themes, A Medieval Wordbook or A Book of Hours. Crumpled and smoothed foil and cut paper were used to look like metal and jewels. The students worked on the text and illustrations over several weeks. There were about twenty students in the class, and we did the covers and sewing in a little under two hours. The sewing and final assembly were done in small groups of three to four students.

Materials:

8 1/2" x 11" white paper

Light cardboard, 5 1/2" x 8 1/2"

Colored paper, 8 1/2" x 10"

Colored paper, 5 1/2" x 11"

Colored paper, 8 1/4" x 2"

White heavy thread in 20" lengths

Aluminum foil, about
10" x 12", torn from 12" roll

Colored paper for collage

Tools:

Pencil

Black and colored markers

Pattern for cutting foil, 5" x 8"

Scissors

Glue stick and scrap paper

Tapestry needles

Push pins or thumbtacks and
scrap cardboard

Clothespins or paper clips

Materials per student:

4 to 7 sheets of 8 1/2" x 11"
white paper

2 pieces 5 1/2" x 8 1/2" light cardboard

2 pieces 8 1/2" x 10" colored paper

2 pieces 5 1/2" x 11" colored paper

1 piece 8 1/4" x 2" colored paper

To Prepare Ahead

1. Make patterns for cutting the foil. Cut light cardboard or heavy paper into 5" x 8" pieces. Write on the pattern: Trace and cut two pieces per book. The project will go more quickly if there are several patterns.

2. Write drafts of the text. Two suggestions for themes are A Medieval Word Book with descriptions of people and objects in medieval life, such as castle, knight, moat, joust, and feast, or A Book of Hours with descriptions of common activities in each month or season of the year. It can describe medieval seasonal customs or be a personal record of one's own favorite activities during the year.

3. Figure out the number of sheets of paper needed. This is the tricky part of this kind of binding. Every sheet of paper gives you four pages. For this book, the writing is done only on the right-facing, or recto, page. The first and last two pages (one sheet of paper) will be blank; these will become part of the cover. Four sheets of paper give blank pages for the front and back covers, a title page, and five pages of text. Five sheets of paper yield the blank pages for the covers, a title page, and seven pages of text.

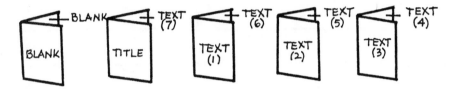

To do A Book of Hours with a title page and twelve pages of text, one for each month, you will need eight sheets of paper.

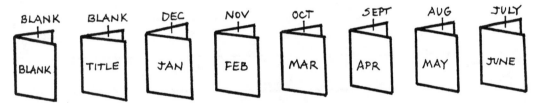

Making the Book

1. Fold the sheets of white paper in half, one sheet at a time.

2. One sheet will be left blank to insert in the front and back covers. The corners are trimmed to make it easier. To do this, take one folded sheet. Mark it with pencil 1/2" from the top and bottom on the open edge. Cut through both pages from the 1/2" marks to the top and bottom edges at the center fold. Set aside until Step 5.

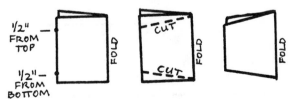

Line Guide

3. Stack the rest of the pages, one sheet inside the other. Number the pages in the bottom corner lightly with a pencil. The numbers are for reference and will be erased.

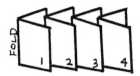

4. Write the text on the pages. Use the pencil numbers to make sure you are writing on the correct pages. Use the line guide if you wish. Photocopy the line guide. Place it under the page. Do the writing on the lines that show through or trace over the lines in pencil. If the paper slips off the line guide, tape them together with masking tape. Be gentle when you pull off the tape.

The square is for a large initial letter, and the lines are for the text. There are many possibilities for designing the pages. The space around the letters can be decorated with pictures or patterns. The picture can go over the edge of the square as the dragon does here. The letter itself can be decorated with patterns, as in the A. The square space can contain only a picture, such as a castle. Many of the books about knights and medieval times can offer ideas for illustrations and designs.

CASTLE

5. Stack the pages in their proper order. The trimmed blank sheet will be on the outside, so that the first and last pages will be blank and trimmed. Check again to make sure they are correct.

6. Hold the stack in both hands and tap against the table so that the paper is even. Clip the top and bottom at the fold with clothespins or paper clips. The book will stay clipped together until the sewing is finished.

7. Pierce three holes along the fold, one in the center, one about 1/2" from the top, and one about 1/2" from the bottom. The holes can be measured and marked first with pencil or just done by eye. Use a thumbtack or push pin to make the holes. Place a piece of cardboard underneath to protect the table.

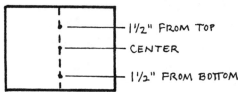

8. To sew the pages together:
    a. Thread the needle. Do not tie a knot. The thread will be used singly, as in embroidery.
    b. Start on the outside of the book at the center hole. Go through the center hole. Pull the thread through, leaving about 6" of thread remaining.

    c. Go to and through the top hole. The top hole will be entered from the inside of the book. Be careful not to pull the thread all the way through. It may help to hold the 6" of thread with your finger.

d. Go to and through the bottom hole. The bottom hole will be entered from the outside of the book.

e. Go to and through the center hole again. The center hole will be entered from the inside of the book.

f. Remove the needle. Arrange the two ends so that one end is on each side of the thread that runs along the center. Tie the two ends in a square knot at the center hole. A square knot is a double knot. The first knot is made with the thread in your right hand on top; the second knot is made with the thread in your left hand on top. A diagram can be found on page 17 in the basic techniques section. Trim the ends so that each end is about 1" long.

9. Erase the page numbers that you made in pencil.

10. To attach the narrow strip of colored paper to the book pages:
    a. Fold the strip in half vertically.
    b. Open and cover the entire piece with glue. Go over the edges and onto the scrap paper.
    c. Place the strip over the spine (the sewn fold) of the book so that the fold of the strip is on top of the fold of the pages. The strip is slightly shorter than the pages and should be centered on the pages. Pressing firmly, run your hand along the spine to adhere.

11. To make the front and back covers: For each cover, you will need one piece of 5 1/2" x 8 1/2" cardboard, one long piece (5 1/2" by 11") of colored paper, and one short piece (8 1/2" x 10") of colored paper. The long piece of paper is the same width as the cardboard. The short piece of paper is the same height as the cardboard.

a. Hold the cardboard vertically. Place it on the tall piece of colored paper so that the sides are even, and there is 1 1/4" of colored paper on the top and bottom. Fold the top and bottom edges of colored paper over the cardboard to make two flaps. Run your fingernail along the edge to crease well.

b. Place the short piece of colored paper horizontally on the table. Place the wrapped cardboard, folded flaps down, on the colored paper so that the tops and bottoms are even, and there is 2 3/4" of colored paper on each side. Fold the side edges of the paper over the cardboard and crease well to make two flaps.

c. Open up the flaps. Trim the four corners on a diagonal from 1" down the edge to the fold.

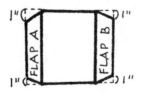

d. Apply glue to Flap A. Go over the edges and onto the scrap paper.

e. Tuck Flap A between the paper on the other side of the cover and the cardboard. Press firmly to adhere.

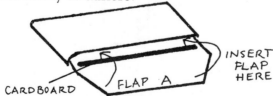

f. Repeat with Flap B. Put your fingers underneath and use your thumbs to push the flap between the paper and the cardboard.

12. To attach the foil to the covers: There are two covers, one for the front of the book and one for the back. Each cover has an outside and an inside. The outside of the cover is the one with the paper wrapped around the sides. The inside of the cover is the one with the paper wrapped around the top and bottom. The foil will go on the outside of the cover.

a. Two pieces will be cut from the foil using the pattern. Fold the foil in half. Center the pattern on the foil, trace around it, and cut.

b. Optional: Gently bunch up the foil, and then smooth it out with the palm of your hand. Do not crumple the foil into a ball. If you do, it will be difficult to smooth it out without tearing it.

c. To glue the foil to the outside of the covers: Decide which side of the foil, shiny or dull, will be face up and apply glue to the other side. Be gentle; the foil can tear easily. It works best if you start at the middle and go to the edges. Use scrap paper underneath and go over the edge of the foil onto the scrap paper. Place the foil, glue side down, on the cover. There will be a border of cover all around. Gently rub the foil all over to adhere.

13. To attach the covers to the pages:

a. Place a piece of scrap paper between an end page and the rest of the pages. Cover the end page with glue. Use scrap paper and go over the edge onto the scrap paper.

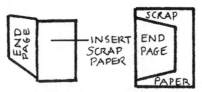

b. Insert your hand between the paper and the cardboard. Arch your fingers to separate the paper from the cardboard.

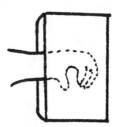

c. Slip the end page between the paper and the cardboard. Push it in until the edge of the cover meets the fold. You may have to wiggle the paper a little to get it in.

d. Press on the cover with your hand to adhere.

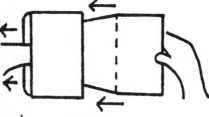

e. Repeat with the other cover.

14. Decorate the front and back covers. A pencil can be used to make indented lines in the foil. Markers can be used to make darker lines. Some markers work better than others. Experiment on a scrap piece of foil. The cover can be divided into sections with lines or boxes, and the sections can be filled in with more lines. Pieces of colored paper can be cut into shapes to serve as jewels. The idea is to make the cover look as if it were covered with silver and jewels.

15. Optional: Cover the front and back covers with clear contact paper to protect them. Use larger pieces of contact paper. Trim the contact paper after attaching it.

Cover Designs

Lines

Boxes

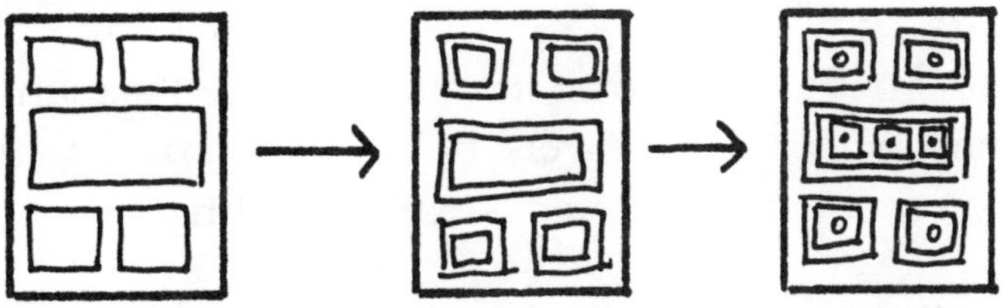

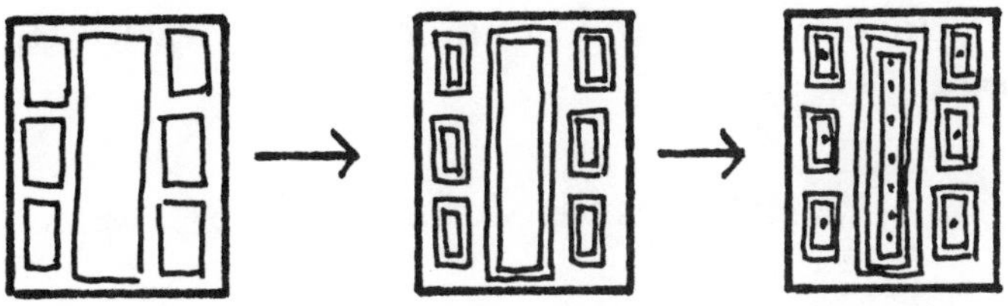

Diamonds
& Triangles

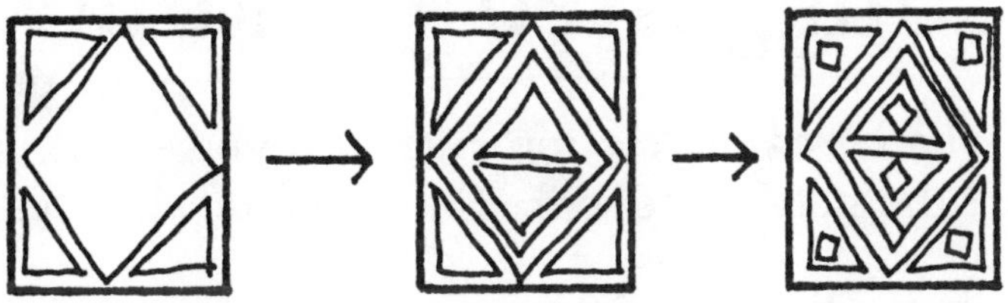

Spirals

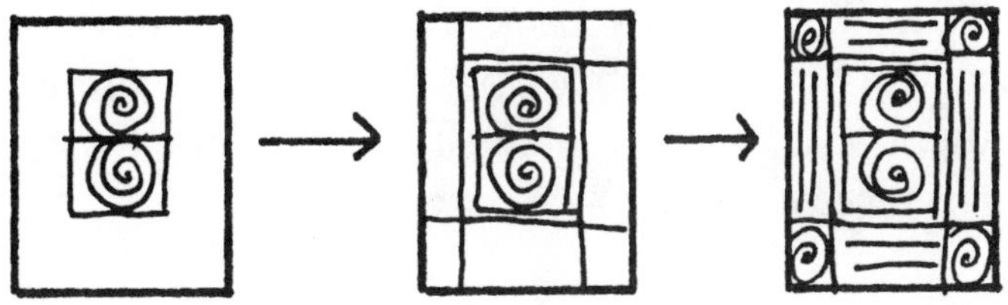

Variations

Use a variety of materials for the cover: Puffy paint, glitter paint, sequins in different sizes and shapes, old beads, rhinestones and plastic jewels from craft stores, and glitter.

Make an easier cover. Use one sheet of heavy paper, 8 3/4" x 11 1/4". Fold it in half and sew it together with the pages. The cover is just slightly larger than the pages.

Make blank books with the easier covers to use for journals and notes. Use patterned paper for the covers, or make patterned paper with potato prints, crayon rubbings of different textures, or fingerpainting.

Bestiaries (books about animals) and Herbiaries (books about plants) were made in medieval times. Use in conjunction with the study of animals or plants.

Make a book of magic spells for Merlin.

Suggested Readings

The Man Who Loved Books, Jean Fritz. New York: G. P. Putnam's Sons, 1981. This is the story of the scribe St. Columba, who loved books.

The Sailor Who Captured the Sea, Deborah Nourse Lattimore. New York: HarperCollins Publishers, 1991. In this story about the Book of Kells from Ireland, three brothers leave their trades to become scribes in the belief that the completion of the book will save their people from the Viking invaders.

Knights of the Kitchen Table, John Scieszka. New York: Viking, 1991. The Time Warp Trio journey back into the time of King Arthur after opening a magical book. This book has the same irreverent humor as John Scieszka's other books, which include *The True Story of the Three Little Pigs* and *The Stinky Cheese Man*.

Any of the many versions of the King Arthur legends.

Directory of Forms

There are six basic book forms used in the projects: scroll, accordion, palm leaf, slat, Oriental stitched binding, and Western stitched binding. This Directory gives a brief overview of cultures and materials, as well as their important features and limitations.

Scroll

Cultures and Materials:
Egypt, Greece, and Rome: papyrus
Israel, Ethiopia, Islamic Africa: leather and vellum
Native Americans; India: birch bark
China, Japan, Korea: silk and paper
Features: Interesting form representing many cultures
Limitations: Awkward to handle and store

Accordion

Cultures and Materials:
Aztecs and Mayans of Mexico and Central America: amate (bark paper) and deerskin
Otomi Indians of San Pablito, Mexico (near Mexico City): amate
China, Japan, Korea, Thailand, Burma: paper
Ethiopia: vellum
Features: Excellent for display as they can be opened to show all the pages at once.
Limitations: Large-format books need a lot of gluing to attach pages

Palm Leaf

Cultures and Materials:
India, Indonesia, Southeast Asia: palm leaves
Indonesia: bamboo
Southeast Asia: ivory, metal, cloth inlaid with mother-of-pearl
India, Southeast Asia: paper
Tibet: unattached paper pages
Features: Excellent for sequencing
Limitations: Less useful for long texts

Slat

Cultures and Materials:
China: wood and bamboo
Features: Excellent for sequencing and wall displays
Limitations: Younger students are unable to make the book on their own.

Oriental Stitched Binding

Cultures and Materials:
China, Japan, Korea, Vietnam: paper
Features: Separate pages make it easy to plan and to discard mistakes. Unfamiliar quality and ease of the binding makes it appealing to students. Most compatible form with pages generated on the computer
Limitations: Binding best done in small groups.

Western Stitched Binding

Cultures and Materials:
Medieval Europe, Iran (Persia), Ethiopia; Copts of
Egypt: vellum and parchment
Europe, U.S., Iran (Persia): paper
Features: Familiar form
Limitations: The layout must be planned in advance and can be complicated because each sheet of paper yields four pages.

For Further Reading

The following list of books is divided into two categories: Instructional Books, which will teach you more about making books, and Historical Information, which will give you more background on the variety of book forms found around the world. They are arranged in what I perceive to be their order of usefulness.

Instructional Books

Creative Bookbinding, Pauline Johnson. New York: Dover Books, 1963, pb. Lots of information on simple bindings and folders, and a large section on printing techniques for covers and endpapers. The best how-to book for school projects.

Japanese Bookbinding, Instructions from a Master Craftsman, Kojiro Ikegami. New York: Weatherhill, 1986, hc. A beautiful book containing clear instructions with photographs and many styles of authentic Japanese bindings. The real thing from a Japanese master.

Non-adhesive Binding, Keith A. Smith. New York: The Sigma Foundation, 1991, pb. Order from: Keith A. Smith, 22 Cayuga St., Rochester, NY 14620. Excellent book with a wealth of information and book forms. Much of the information will be too advanced for children, but there is some worthwhile material.

Paper Pleasures, Faith Shannon. New York: Weidenfeld & Nicolson, 1987, hc. How to create with paper, including books. Beautifully designed and illustrated. Instructions are a bit vague at times, but presentation is inspirational.

The Haiku Handbook: How to Write, Share, and Teach Haiku, William J. Higginson with Penny Harter. New York: McGraw-Hill Book Company, 1985, pb. A thorough guide to writing and teaching haiku, with chapters on "Haiku for Kids" and "A Lesson Plan that Works."

How to Make Pop-ups, Joan Irvine. New York: Morrow Junior Books, 1987, pb. Just as the title says. Basics of pop-up construction in card format with information on how to assemble them in book form at the end. The pop-up sections can also be glued into accordion books.

Historical Information

"Paper" Through the Ages, Shaaron Cosner. Minneapolis: Carolrhoda Books, 1984. A beginning reader on a variety of writing surfaces throughout history, including stone, clay, papyrus, wax, parchment and paper.

Books and Libraries, Jack Knowlton. New York: Harper Collins Publishers, 1991. Children's book on the history of books and libraries. Emphasis on Western forms, from Mesopotamia and Egypt to Europe and colonial New England.

Book, Karen Brookfield. New York: Alfred A. Knopf, 1993, hc. One of the Eyewitness Books series. Beautifully illustrated with photographs. Not comprehensive and weighted towards Western books, but full of treasures nonetheless. Recommended.

The Book Before Printing: Ancient, Medieval and Oriental, David Diringer. New York: Dover Publications, 1982, pb. Dover reprint of work originally published as *The Hand-Produced Book* in 1953. Reference book on the history of handmade books. Good resource, although its 563 pages may tell you more than you want to know.

A History of Writing, Albertine Gaur. New York: Cross River Press, a Division of Abbeville Press, 1992, pb. Primary focus on the developments of alphabets and scripts, but good information on book forms as well.

Bibliography

Asihene, Emmanuel V., *Understanding the Traditional Art of Ghan.*, Rutherford, NJ: Fairleigh Dickinson University Press, 1978.

Barker, Nicolas, *Treasures of the British Library*. New York: Harry N. Abrams, Inc., 1988.

Brookfield, Karen, *Book*. New York: Alfred A. Knopf, 1993.

Diringer, David, *The Book Before Printing: Ancient, Medieval and Oriental*. New York: Dover Publications, 1982.

Emmerich, Andre, *Art Before Columbus*. New York: Simon & Schuster, 1963.

Gaur, Albertine, *A History of Writing*. New York: Cross River Press, 1992.

Guar, Albertine, *Writing Materials of the East*. London: The British Library, 1979.

Guojun, Liu and Zheng Rusi, *The Story of Chinese Books*. Beijing, Foreign Languages Press: 1985.

Henry, David J., *Beyond Words:The Art of the Book*. Rochester, New York: Memorial Art Gallery, University of Rochester, 1986.

Jackson, Donald, *The Story of Writing*. New York: Taplinger Publishing Co., Inc, 1981.

Jolles, Frank, "Traditional Zulu Beadwork of the Msinga Area," *African Arts*, vol. 25, no. 1, pp. 42-53, Los Angeles, J.S. Coleman African Studies Center, University of California, January 1993.

Mack, John, ed. *Ethnic Jewelry*, NY, Harry N. Abrams, Inc., 1988.

Martinique, Edward, *Chinese Traditional Bookbinding: A Study of Its Evolution and Techniques*, Republic of China, Chinese Materials Center, 1983.

McMurtrie, Douglas C., *The Book: The Story of Printing and Bookmaking*, NY, Dorset Press, 1943.

Mercier, Jacques, *Ethiopian Magic Scrolls*. New York: George Braziller, 1979.

Page, R. I., *Runes*. Berkeley, CA: University of California Press, 1987.

Quarcoo, A. K., *The Language of Adinkra Patterns*. Legon, Ghana: Institute of African Studies, University of Ghana, 1972.

Sayer, Chloe, *Arts and Crafts of Mexico*. San Francisco: Chronicle Books, 1990.

Schuman, Jo Miles, *Art from Many Hands: Multicultural Art Projects*. Worcerster, MA: Davis Publications, Inc, 1981.

Steffens, Bradley, *Printing Press: Ideas in Type*. San Diego: Lucent Books, 1990.

Tsien, Tsuen-hsuin, *Written on Bamboo and Silk*. Chicago: University of Chicago Press, 1962.

Ullman, B. L., *Ancient Writing and Its Influence*. Toronto: University of Toronto Press, 1980.